T0065922

GUITARIST'S GUIDE TO

ECONOMY PICKING

Learn to Play Fast, Lean, and Clean with the Picking Techniques of the Masters

by Chad Johnson

PLAYBACK+
Speed • Pitch • Balance • Loop

ISBN 978-1-4950-7091-4

7777 W. BLUEMOUND RD. P.O. BOX 13819 MILWAUKEE, WI 53213

In Australia Contact:
Hal Leonard Australia Pty. Ltd.
4 Lentara Court
Cheltenham, Victoria, 3192 Australia
Email: ausadmin@halleonard.com.au

Visit Hal Leonard Online at
www.halleonard.com

CONTENTS

PAGE

4   Introduction

4   About the Author

5   How to Use This Book

6   Recommended Listening

9   SECTION 1: GETTING STARTED

9   Chapter 1 – The Basics

16   Chapter 2 – Technical Concerns

26   Chapter 3 – Three-Notes-Per-String Scales

31   SECTION 2: SPECIFIC APPLICATIONS

31   Chapter 4 – Repetitive Three-Note Patterns

38   Chapter 5 – Repetitive Four-Note Patterns

45   Chapter 6 – Adding Legato

52   Chapter 7 – Extended Sweep Picking

64   SECTION 3: THE BIG PICTURE

64   Chapter 8 – Licks and Tricks of the Masters

70   Chapter 9 – Full Solo Examples

74   Afterword

75   Appendix

INTRODUCTION

Welcome to *Guitarist's Guide to Economy Picking*. If you're reading this book, you're no doubt curious about this interesting subject. Perhaps you have no experience with it whatsoever and are intrigued by the possibilities. Maybe you've heard/read that one of your favorite players uses economy picking and you'd like to be able to do what he/she does. Or maybe you've dabbled in it already but aren't sure when, where, and how to apply it. In any of those cases, you've come to the right place.

In many circles, there are quite spirited debates about guitar technique, and picking is no exception. Many people will tell you how you're supposed to hold the pick, which motion or angle you should use when picking, which direction to pick on certain beats (or subdivisions of the beat), etc. I'm not going to get into that debate here. The way I see it, history has more than demonstrated that there's no one right way to do it. If you look at 10 different shredders, you'll most likely see at least five different picking methods (if not more). I attribute this to the fact that everyone's hands, arms, and fingers are different, so why try to apply a one-size-fits-all mentality to the subject?

Economy picking is an exciting technique that allows you to do some pretty amazing things on the instrument—things that would be extremely difficult (or just outright impossible) with alternate picking alone. This is, of course, not to say that one method is better than the other; on the contrary, both have their uses—not to mention strengths and weaknesses—and many players employ both on a regular basis. So, although this book concentrates solely on the economy picking technique, please don't infer that I'm suggesting it replace your alternate picking technique. While some players do decide to make economy picking their primary technique, that's a decision that's entirely up to the individual. Personally, I make use of both techniques in my playing, depending on the phrase at hand, and that approach works well for me.

It's my hope that you'll find the exercises in this book enjoyable and effective. I tried my best to accomplish this and had a great time doing so.

—Chad Johnson

ABOUT THE AUTHOR

Chad Johnson is a freelance author, editor, and musician. For Hal Leonard Corporation, he's authored over 70 instructional books covering a variety of instruments and topics, including *Guitarist's Guide to Scales Over Chords*, *How to Fingerpick Songs on Guitar*, *How to Record at Home on a Budget*, *Teach Yourself to Play Bass Guitar*, *Ukulele Aerobics*, *Pentatonic Scales for Guitar: The Essential Guide*, *Pink Floyd Signature Licks*, *Play Like Robben Ford*, and *Play Like Eric Johnson*, to name but a few. He's a featured instructor on the DVD *200 Country Guitar Licks* (also published by Hal Leonard) and has toured and performed throughout the East Coast in various bands, sharing the stage with members of Lynyrd Skynyrd, the Allman Brothers Band, Jamey Johnson, and others. He works as a session instrumentalist, composer/songwriter, and recording engineer when not authoring or editing and also enjoys tinkering with electronics. Chad currently resides in Denton, TX with his wife and two children. Feel free to contact him at *chadjohnsonguitar@gmail.com* with any questions or concerns; you can also connect with him at *www.facebook.com/chadjohnsonguitar* to hear about his latest book releases and other musical adventures.

HOW TO USE THIS BOOK

Guitarist's Guide to Economy Picking is divided into three sections. It's organized as a method, as opposed to a reference, so it's highly recommended that you progress through the entire book from front to back. For those of you who are already familiar with the technique, the early chapters may seem elementary. Nonetheless, I'd still recommend at least skimming through them to make sure that you're up to speed on any unique terminology I may be using—not to mention the fact that a little review never hurt anybody!

- **Section 1:** In this section, we introduce the basic idea of the technique with some simple examples. We're starting at ground zero here for those of you who have no idea what the technique involves. We'll address some common roadblocks that many players encounter when trying this technique for the first time. This includes alternate pickers who are looking to employ some economy picking in their playing. We'll wrap up the section with a look at one of the most ubiquitous applications of this technique: playing scales with three notes per string.

- **Section 2:** In this section, we'll look at several specific applications for the technique that capitalize on different aspects of it. Some of these are the types of licks for which some players employ the economy technique naturally—they simply gravitate toward it without even giving it much thought. Others will be more calculated uses. We'll also look at how the technique can be mixed with legato in ways that help relieve the burden on the pick hand while also providing a different timbre. And when you take economy picking to the extreme, you get *sweep picking*, and that's the final focus of the section. We'll begin with shorter three-string sweeps and progress to the full range. Interestingly, many players who employ sweep picking are otherwise strict alternate pickers with regard to scalar playing. There are likely reasons for this, which we'll talk about along the way.

- **Section 3:** In the final section, we'll put it all together with some examples that are written in the styles of the masters of the technique (most of whom are listed in the Recommended Listening section). These types of lines are often very revealing of a player's technical tendencies—i.e., the ideas they gravitate toward or shy away from—so it's usually an enlightening process. We'll finish off with a few full-length solo examples that tie together all the ideas presented in the book.

UPS AND DOWNS

Terminology such as "up/down," "high/low," etc. can get a bit confusing at times as it applies to the guitar, so I'd like to make it clear up front so we're all on the same page. It surprises me how often I hear guitarists refer to their strings backwards. So, to clarify:

String 6 (the **low** E) = the thickest, lowest-pitched string; nearest to the ceiling while in playing position.
String 1 (the **high** E) = the thinnest, highest-pitched string; nearest to the floor while in playing position.

Additional confusion is possible when talking about direction of sweeps as opposed to the direction of a musical phrase. When I talk about a downward sweep, or *downstroke*, I'm talking about moving the pick toward the floor; conversely, an upward sweep, or *upstroke*, is moving the pick toward the ceiling. When I talk about a phrase ascending, or moving from low to high, I'm talking about musical pitch.

Also, note that I may use the terms "economy" and "sweep" interchangeably at times. For instance, when I refer to a "sweep," I'm talking about an instance of economy picking.

It's About Time

It is *highly* recommended that you work through this book with a metronome or drum machine, as tempo is one of the big problem areas that many players encounter when trying this technique for the first time. While learning the coordination in the beginning, it's very easy to produce a lopsided sound as you move from one string to the next. Try not to be discouraged if it takes a while to get the hang of it; if you've done nothing but alternate pick so far, it most likely will be slow-going at first. Try to dedicate at least 30 minutes a day to this book if you want to see results. The technical advancement you'll attain is well worth the effort! Good luck!

RECOMMENDED LISTENING

If you want to hear what the economy picking technique can do, look (or listen) no further than the following list of players. They all make extensive use of it in at least one capacity, and the results speak for themselves.

Frank Gambale

The fusion master from Down Under is pretty much the poster boy for economy picking. He's based his entire style around the technique and generally employs it whenever it's possible to do so. His instructional video from 1992, *Monster Licks and Speed Picking* (re-released on DVD in 2000), is an excellent resource for viewing his awesome technique up close and personal. He's also released other videos since, including *Modes: No More Mystery* and *Chop Builder*. Check out *Thunder from Down Under* (1990) or his work with Chick Corea's Elektric Band to hear him in a fusion setting, or listen to *The Great Explorers* (1993) to hear him rock out a bit more. *Coming to Your Senses* (2000) straddles the rock/fusion fence, perhaps leaning a bit more to the fusion side, and contains some stellar playing as well.

Eric Johnson

As we'll see throughout this book, economy picking is not an all-or-nothing venture, and many players only apply one facet of it. Eric is a prime example of this, as he generally only uses the technique with downstrokes. Save for the occasional backwards rake, Eric has engineered his lines so that he either changes strings after an upstroke (with which he can move to a higher or lower string) or he employs a downstroke sweep to move from a lower-pitched string to a higher-pitched one. It's really quite interesting how much he adheres to this M.O., often employing fret-hand stretches to play notes on a different string than normal to maintain it. Although he doesn't specifically mention it, you can see it on display (you may have to engage slow motion) in his excellent instructional videos *Total Electric Guitar* (1990) and *The Fine Art of Guitar* (1996), as well as his famous performance at Austin City Limits, *Live from Austin, TX* (recorded in 1988 but released in 2005). His Grammy-winning *Ah Via Musicom* (1990), as well as *Tones* (1986) and *Venus Isle* (1996), are essential listening for any fan.

Joe Pass

Although he became increasingly known for his fingerstyle chord-melody approach in his later days, the late, great jazz master was also a fierce picker in his earlier years. Similarly to Eric, he generally only made use of the technique with downstrokes. He stated in his instructional video *Jazz Lines* (1991) that he always began with a downstroke on a new string. He would employ a downward sweep when moving from a low-pitched to high-pitched string if possible. Otherwise, he would employ hammer-ons or pull-offs to always allow him to start with a downstroke on a new string. I'm not sure if he always applied this logic (always starting with a downstroke on a new string), because in an early video of him from what appears to be the '60s (on which he's playing a Fender Jaguar), he certainly seems to be picking a lot (as opposed to employing lots of legato slurs). Nevertheless, it's clearly evident in many videos that he did employ downward sweeps often, and that concurs with his statement. By the way, you can find the aforementioned video on YouTube by searching "Joe Pass Fender Jaguar," and it's highly recommended you do! Also check out his seminal recordings *Virtuoso* (1973) and *Intercontinental* (1970) to hear the master in action.

Marshall Harrison

Probably the least known player in this list, Marshall Harrison has begun showing up on the radar of some players largely due to his YouTube videos, nearly all of which feature jaw-dropping technical displays. Similar to Gambale, Marshall is pretty much an exclusive economy picker. He's also extremely adept at legato technique, able to mimic Allan Holdsworth-style fusion lines with ease. Check out his YouTube channel (simply search "Marshall Harrison guitar") for many in-depth lessons and awe-inspiring displays of his formidable technique.

Yngwie Malmsteen

The Swedish shredmaster has a technique that's similar to Eric Johnson's in that he tends to employ economy picking only on downstrokes. He also tends to change strings only after an upstroke or, if moving from a lower-pitched string to a higher one, with a downward sweep. For example, he'll use economy picking to pick ascending scales in a three-notes-per-string method (although he doesn't tend to be as formulaic with this as some players are), but if he's descending a three-notes-per-string scale, he'll usually pick down, pick up, and then pull-off the final note on each string. This method—pick-pick-pull when descending three notes per string—allows him to end each string with an upstroke (which is followed by a pull-off). Although he doesn't really slow down much for you, you can see his technique close up in his self-titled instructional video from 1991 if you're handy with the slow-motion feature. Essential listening includes *Rising Force* (1984), *Trilogy* (1986), *Odyssey* (1988), and *Eclipse* (1990).

Zakk Wylde

Zakk is another player who makes use of the "only on downstrokes" brand of economy picking. Like Eric Johnson, Zakk loves his pentatonic scales and can shred them to pieces, employing similar tricks in that regard. He also mixes in a good bit of hybrid picking (something he also has in common with E.J.) to get some hyper-speed chicken-pickin' sounds. Check out his instructional video, *Pentatonic Hardcore* (1996), to see his dizzying technique in action. Essential listening includes the Ozzy albums *No Rest for the Wicked* (1988) and *No More Tears* (1991), along with his work in Black Label Society. What's even more impressive about Zakk is the way he never seems to get his fingers caught in his hair, which seems to be perpetually falling onto his fretboard!

Jason Becker

Gaining early notoriety on the Shrapnel label with his solo album *Perpetual Burn* in 1988 (as well as his work with Marty Friedman in Cacophony), Jason was a scary player at a very young age. His career seemed to be headed for the high ground when he replaced Steve Vai in David Lee Roth's band for the *A Little Ain't Enough* album (1991). While recording the guitars for the album, however, the first signs of the debilitating disease, A.L.S., began to surface. Tragically, his guitar-playing career was cut short, and by 1996, he had lost the ability to speak. Originally given a prognosis of three-to-five years to live, his mind remains sharp to this day, and he still composes music with the aid of a computer. Becker was one of the most accomplished arpeggio sweep-pickers ever to hold a pick and would occasionally employ economy picking for certain scalar lines as well.

Jeff Loomis

Jeff gained fame with the progressive metal band Nevermore, with which he played from 1992 to 2014. Loomis can alternate pick and economy pick with staggering precision, and he's also an amazingly smooth sweep picker of extended arpeggio shapes. He released an instructional video with *Guitar World* magazine called *Super Shred Guitar: Master Class* (Alfred) in 2009, and you can also see many up-close examples of his technique on YouTube, as he's featured in many equipment demonstrations and the like. Check out Nevermore's self-titled album from 1995, *Dead Heart in a Dead World* (2000), and *This Godless Endeavor* (2005) to hear some classic examples of his formidable shredding.

Honorable Mentions

There are many other players that employ sweep picking but tend to resort to mostly alternate picking (or legato) for the bulk of their scalar lines. Here are but a few:

- Michael Romeo
- Greg Howe
- Michael Angelo Batio
- Richie Kotzen

- John Petrucci
- Tony MacAlpine
- Vinnie Moore
- Jimmy Bruno

- Morten Faerestrand
- Barney Kessel
- Grant Green

SECTION 1: GETTING STARTED
CHAPTER 1 – THE BASICS

Before we get underway, I want to reiterate that I'm in no way suggesting that economy picking is superior (or inferior) to alternate picking. Nor am I suggesting that you should replace your alternate picking technique entirely with economy picking. Since you bought this book, however, I assume you want to learn how to economy pick, so I'll present the benefits as I see them. Personally, I use both methods (alternate and economy) hand in hand, as I think that represents the best of both worlds and widens your aperture of playable lines as a guitarist. In my humble opinion, there are some instances in which alternate picking makes more sense, and there are other times where economy picking does. So why not make use of both? Interestingly, although I was well aware of economy picking for a good while, it was the act of learning to play bass that made me consider it on guitar. With bass playing (plucking with the fingers), you're taught right away to always "rake" or "drag" a finger from one string to the next whenever possible, as opposed to always alternating your index and middle fingers, for instance. This is kind of equivalent to economy picking with the plectrum. Learning to do that on the bass made me realize that both techniques (alternate and economy) can easily exist side by side. For whatever reason, that clicked for me and sparked my interest in using the technique for guitar.

I'd also like to address the two main concerns that plague many players in regard to economy picking. One comment I often hear is that alternate picking is already too engrained in their playing to learn a new method. In other words, "You can't teach an old dog new tricks." To that, I simply say "bollocks!" (Or I would if I were British.) I used alternate picking exclusively for nearly 25 years, and I was able to begin seriously implementing economy picking into my technique within a period of three or four months. Another concern is that it will confuse you or trip you up if you try to have both methods coexist in your technique. Again, from personal experience, I haven't found this to be true at all. You simply learn to think ahead with regard to your picking in the same way you do with your fretting. With practice, it's easy to drift from alternate picking to economy picking and back all within the scope of one lick.

Now, with that said, let's get on with it. We'll start our journey with a description of what we mean by the term *economy picking*. Although the term is not completely standardized in the guitar world—some don't make a distinction between economy and sweep picking, for example, and I've heard others use the terms *directional picking* or *continuous picking*—the generally accepted idea is that economy picking refers to the act of continuing a pick stroke to an adjacent string whenever possible. For example, if you're picking a note on string 6 with a downstroke, and the next note in on string 5, you'd simply continue the same downstroke motion through both strings. This is opposed to alternate picking, whereby you would pick down on string 6 and up on string 5.

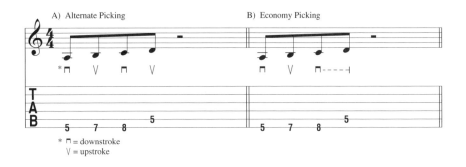

Notice in the above example that there aren't two separate downstroke symbols (⊓) for the last two notes of Example B. That because it's one downstroke motion that continues through both strings. Making two separate downstroke motions will defeat the purpose, which is to eliminate excess picking motion.

With descending lines, the same principle applies. Here's another comparison of the two methods, this time in descending fashion:

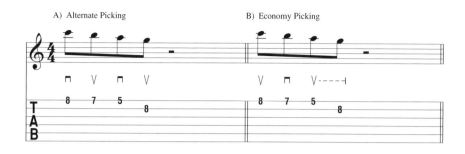

Here we can see the first major departure (if we call the ascending example a minor departure) in picking between the two methods. In order to employ economy picking in a descending fashion for this lick, we need to *start on an upstroke* so that the third (and last) note on string 1 is an upstroke, too. This is a significant difference between the two methods, and we'll look more closely at it in Chapter 2.

OLD HABITS DIE HARD

For me personally, the idea of starting a phrase on an upstroke like this was one of the biggest hurdles I had to overcome when learning to economy pick. As a purely alternate picker for so long, I tended to always pair downstrokes with downbeats and upstrokes with upbeats. It's not as though I would never begin a phrase with an upstroke—I usually would if it were occurring in between the beats. There would be the occasional exception where I might, for example, play a bluesy lick by picking up on string 1, down on string 2, and then pulling off, but I would hardly ever begin a completely picked phrase on a *downbeat* with an *upstroke*. So when it came time to do this with economy picking, it took a *lot* of getting used to.

I have a friend who's a fabulous player who taught himself to economy pick from the beginning, simply because it made more sense to him. But if you're like me and experience the same type of trouble, all I can say is: don't fret it. With slow practice, the coordination will develop. And the results are definitely worth it!

Boot Camp Drills

For now, let's get our feet wet with a few easy drills that isolate the technique. Start very slowly and don't move on until the rhythm is solid (and not lopsided at all) throughout. For simplicity's sake, these examples will all be in the key of C. We're not making great art yet, so don't read too much into the musical content (or lack thereof) in these drills. We're just getting used to the feeling on each group of adjacent strings.

Example 1

TRACK 1

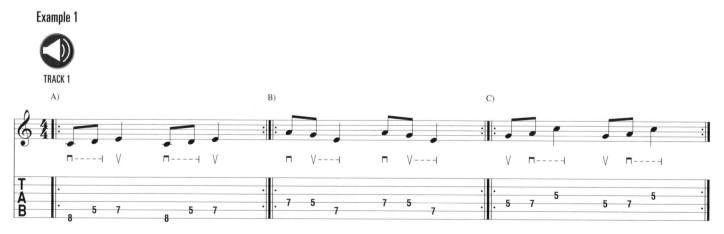

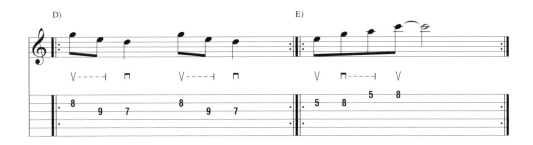

Again, be sure that you're not using two distinct motions for the sweeps. In Example A above, for instance, it's OK at this point if your pick comes to rest against string 5 a bit early (after picking string 6 on beat 1 with a downstroke) and has to wait there for a fraction of a second before you pick the D note at fret 5, string 5. What you *don't* want is the pick to lift back up again to restrike that D note.

Now let's look at some eighth-note drills that you can loop continuously. Here, we're using both downward and upward sweeps. Again, pay close attention to the picking directions; that's the entire point here.

Example 2

TRACK 2

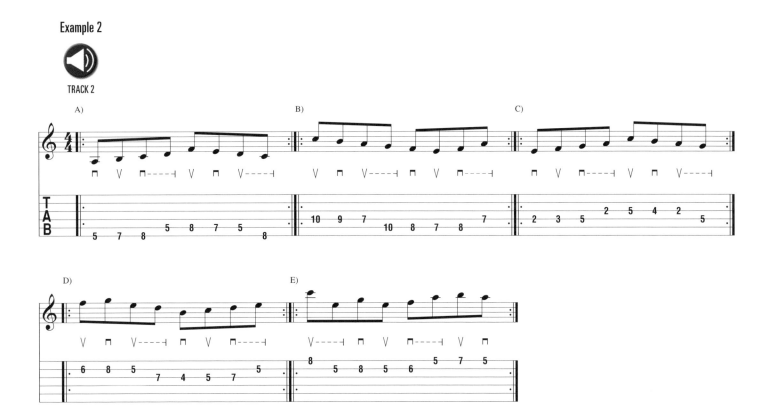

And now let's try some triplet examples—again, using both downward and upward sweeps.

Example 3

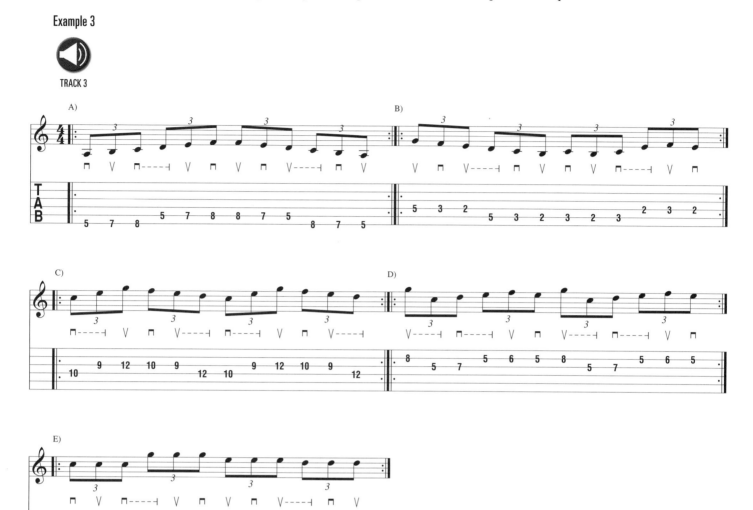

TRACK 3

Again, starting on an upstroke for the downbeat can certainly feel odd if you're not used to it. It helped me to work on some exercises with regards to this. Here are a few that were particularly useful to me. Pay very close attention to the picking directions here. Again, these aren't musical masterpieces (i.e., they're not that fun), but the coordination gained is important.

Example 4

TRACK 4

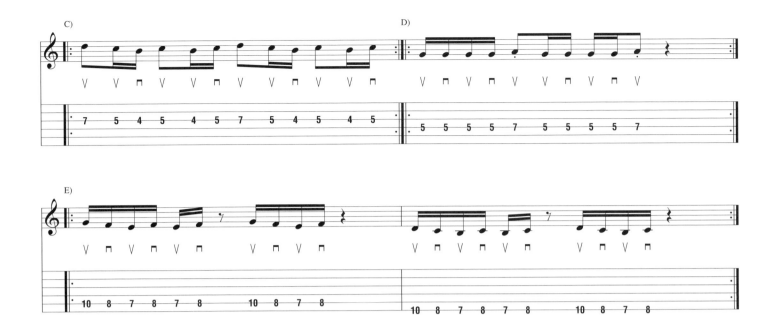

And now let's mix it up a bit. We're starting some beats on downstrokes and some on upstrokes. Again, adhere to the picking directions on these, as they're the whole point of the exercises.

Example 5

TRACK 5

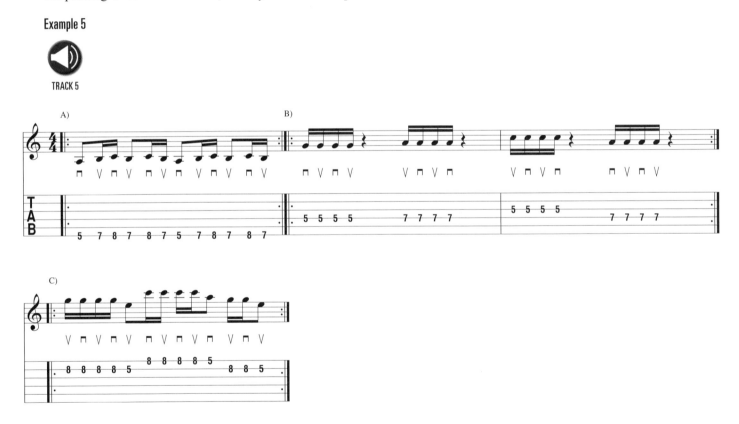

Your First Economy Picking Licks

Let's close out the chapter with a few "baby step" licks that make sparse use of economy picking in an applicable way. These licks aren't difficult, the tempos are fairly slow, and they usually only feature one or two sweeps, but make extra sure that your timing is solid and the execution is clean. Those are two common errors with any new technique, and economy picking is no different. It's very common for a lick to have a lopsided sound—one note either rushed or dragged—when learning to economy pick, so pay close attention to this. Also make sure that all of the notes are speaking out clearly.

We'll branch out into different keys now that we're actually making some music, but the first lick is from the A minor pentatonic scale. There are just two downstroke sweeps in this one, but make sure the timing is good!

Lick 1

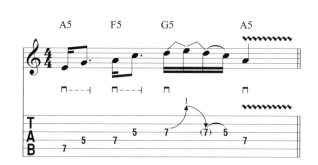

Here's one from B minor pentatonic that uses two upstroke sweeps. Make sure that all four notes in beat 1 are even in rhythm.

Lick 2

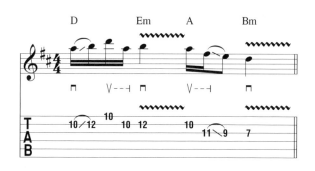

This one, from the A Mixolydian mode, uses one sweep in each direction. Make sure that you're watching the pick directions—and use a metronome!

Lick 3

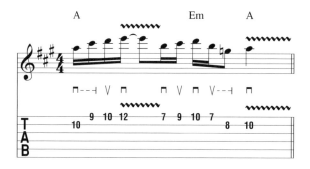

Finally, this one, from C minor pentatonic, uses two sweeps placed in close proximity to each other amidst a 16th-note line. Be sure that this one isn't sounding lopsided at all; the 16th notes should be even throughout.

Lick 4

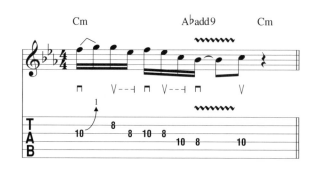

Again, these examples are fairly slow, and therefore you don't really need the economy picking technique (heck—you could probably pick them with downstrokes exclusively at this tempo and be fine). But the point is simply to train your coordination of using the economy technique with solid timing, and timing mistakes are easier to spot at moderate and slow tempos than they are at faster tempos.

WHAT YOU LEARNED

- The term *economy picking* refers to the continuation of one pick stroke to an adjacent one whenever possible. Some people also refer to this as *sweep picking*, *directional picking*, or *continuous picking*.

- Economy picking and alternate picking can coexist! You don't need to use either one exclusively unless you want to.

- Sometimes we need to start a lick on an upstroke to facilitate the economy technique.

- When moving from one string to the next, don't lift your pick up and make a new striking motion. Instead, allow the pick to continue on to the adjacent string with one continuous motion.

- Starting a phrase on a downbeat with an upstroke can feel odd for many players, but you will get used to it.

- When you're starting out, it's common for the technique to sound rhythmically "lopsided." So start slowly and concentrate on keeping steady time.

CHAPTER 2 – TECHNICAL CONCERNS

Now that you've gotten your feet wet a bit in Chapter 1, let's examine things a bit more closely with regard to what's going on technically. It can feel quite odd to the picking hand at first, but there are some things that we can do to make it easier, and that's what this chapter is about.

Pick Angling and/or Slanting

You may have noticed in Chapter 1 that one direction of sweeping felt a little more natural than another. It may have felt awkward both ways, but if it felt as though one direction was fighting you a bit more than another, you're not alone. This usually has to do with how we hold the pick. There are lots of different ways to hold it, and they all have an effect on the way the pick moves through the strings. Some ways will facilitate down-sweeps better, while others will make up-sweeps easier.

Because everyone's hands are different, it's hard to give one-size-fits-all advice in this regard. Generally speaking, however, tilting the top of the pick (the blunt end farthest from the strings) toward the direction of the sweep will usually make it easier. This doesn't have to be a drastic movement—a little bit goes a long way—but you'd be surprised at what a difference it can make. See the photos below for an idea of what I'm talking about.

Forward Pick Slant

*Slanting the pick for a
downward sweep*

Backward Pick Slant

*Slanting the pick for an
upward sweep*

BUT DON'T TAKE MY WORD FOR IT!

Again, you can clearly see this idea at work while watching some economy pickers. Frank Gambale is a prime example, as he clearly changes his pick grip depending on which direction he's headed (it's most obvious in his instructional videos because he's playing straight up and down scales for demonstration purposes).

Interestingly, this is not really the case for players like Yngwie Malmsteen, who only uses economy picking on downstrokes. Both he and Eric Johnson most likely do this because of the way they hold the pick: they both use what I call a "forward pick slant" (see photos above) almost all the time. This means that, after a downstroke, the pick is buried a bit beneath the plane of the strings, so it's difficult to pick the next note with an upstroke if it's on a different string. After an upstroke, however, the pick is floating above the strings, thus making it easier to change to a new string. Of course, this only applies when they're playing at hyper speed. At slower speeds, they can, and will, employ more alternate picking if necessary.

Let's try a few examples to isolate this issue. For each of the following examples, aside from paying strict attention to the picking directions, which applies to this whole book, experiment with your pick angle and slant to see which feels best.

Example 1

TRACK 10

Example 2

TRACK 11

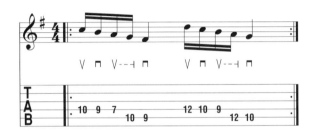

Example 3

TRACK 12

Example 4

TRACK 13

If you're like most people, you'll find it easier to use a forward pick slant for Example 1 throughout. Similarly, you'll find it easiest to use a backward pick slant for Example 2 throughout.

Examples 3 and 4 are a little different, though; they throw a little monkey wrench into things. You'll most likely feel the need to make an adjustment to your pick for the final note in each example. This is perfectly normal, and if you examine the motion slowly, there's really no way around it.

In Example 3, for instance, you're picking the E note at fret 7 at the end of beat 1 with a downstroke, and you have to pick the next note, which is on string 6, with an upstroke. So, you have two options:

1. You can leave your pick at the same angle/slant after picking the E note—which, considering that you just used a downstroke, is most likely in a forward pick slant or a neutral (no slant) position—and backtrack, hopping over string 5 in the process, to pick string 6 with an upstroke.

2. You can move to a backward pick slant after picking the E note—actually, it would likely happen *while* you're picking the E note—which will help you clear string 5 when heading toward string 6 for the upstroke.

Of the two possibilities, the latter is clearly more efficient, and therefore I definitely recommend it. If you feel as though you don't want to abandon your forward pick slant at any time, then you're more than likely going to end up using economy picking primarily for downstrokes, like Yngwie and EJ. Of course, there's nothing wrong with this (it hasn't seemed to hurt those two much), but it means that you're likely going to be making use of some legato moves along the way to accommodate this technique. Again, this is certainly not a bad thing. We'll talk more about this idea of using legato in conjunction with economy picking in Chapter 6.

More Than One Way to Skin a Cat

As we'll see in many spots throughout this book, economy picking doesn't always have to be an all-or-nothing thing; instead, we can choose to employ it on only portions of a lick if it makes sense to do that. The following exercises demonstrate this idea.

This first one is designed to show just how many different ways we can pick a line. Each phrase consists of five notes: four 16th notes and one quarter note. Not counting ways that obviously don't make sense, such as repeating the same stroke direction two times in a row on the same string, there are five different ways to efficiently pick this example, labeled A–E. Be sure to try each one to see how it feels.

Example 5

TRACK 14

Now let's examine each picking strategy in depth.

- **Method A:** This is probably the most common method of all; it's all alternate picking, beginning with a downstroke on the downbeat. If you're a forward pick-slanter, this method most likely works great for you. You pick down on string 2 and then up on string 2. After that upstroke, your pick will be slightly above the plane of the strings (because of the forward pick slant), so it will be fairly easy to move to string 1 and pick the third note with a downstroke. After picking the fourth note with an upstroke on string 1, not only will your pick be above the strings, but you'll also be moving toward string 2, so it's a fairly easy matter to clear string 2 and then use a downstroke for the last note of the phrase.

- **Method B:** This is the opposite of Method A. It's all alternate picking, beginning with an upstroke. It's not nearly as common as Method A, but, assuming you use a backward pick slant, it works just as well. It would prove quite problematic for a forward pick-slanter, though, because the string changes would be fighting you throughout.

- **Method C:** This is one method for employing partial economy picking, particularly for forward pick-slanters. After an initial upstroke on string 2, we push through strings 2 and 1 with one continuous downstroke, which is made easy with forward pick-slanting. We then resume alternate picking for the final two notes: an upstroke on string 1 followed by a downstroke on string 2. It's important to notice that these last two notes are picked the same way as the last two notes in Method A.

- **Method D:** Another choice for partial economy picking, this one is a bit more suited for neutral pickers (no pick slant) or backward pick-slanters. After alternate picking the first four notes, just as in Method A, we continue the upstroke from the fourth note (on string 1) through to the last note (on string 2). You wouldn't want to use a backward pick slant for the first two notes; instead, you would shift to it while picking on string 1. Alternatively, you could use mostly a neutral position throughout.

- **Method E:** This is full economy picking, which means taking advantage of every possibility available. We begin with an upstroke on string 2, push through strings 2 and 1 with one downstroke, and then push through strings 1 and 2 with one upstroke. For this type of lick—one in which you're quickly switching the direction of the sweeps—the neutral position seems to work best.

What did you think? Were some easier than others? Did any of them seem like a complete waste of time? In other words, did you think "I'm never going to use this method" with regard to any of them? These are informative questions to answer.

FORK IN THE ROAD?

This may seem a bit too analytical (i.e., all this discussion for five notes), but I urge you to strongly consider the different options available. This kind of lick represents a bit of a crossroads with regard to how you'd like to employ economy picking into your technique. Do you want to go all-in and use it whenever possible? Or do you want to use it only when it helps you avoid some pitfalls that exist with alternate picking? Experimenting with the five different choices above can help you make that decision—or at least help give you an idea.

For example, although I was an alternate picker (for the most part) for years, and therefore spent over a decade picking this type of example using Method A, I find that Method C actually feels the best to me. Since I spent so much time as an alternate picker with a slight forward pick slant, sweeping with downstrokes definitely felt more natural at first. I've since become very comfortable with sweeping upstrokes, as well, but Method C feels like the best of both worlds to me. It allows me to retain my natural pick slant while also employing some efficiency via a sweep. If I had used more of a backward pick slant all those years prior, this probably wouldn't be the case.

At any rate, the point is that there's no need to sign your life away as an economy picker. What you'll learn, if you continue to develop the technique, is that it will become simply another choice for you, but you won't have to abandon your alternate picking ways. It's like learning how to write cursive. Just because you do it, it doesn't mean you forget how to print. The two skills can coexist and each serves a purpose.

Let's take a look at a few more examples with various picking possibilities. Play through each one, trying out all the picking suggestions and noting which ones feel best or make the most sense.

Example 6

TRACK 15

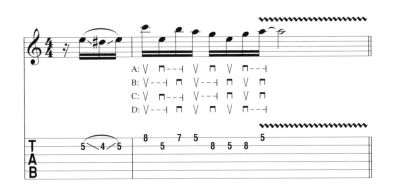

Example 7

TRACK 16

Example 8

TRACK 17

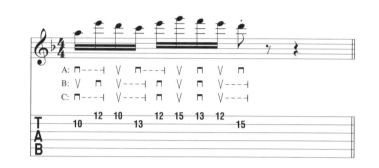

Example 9

TRACK 18

For each of the above examples, the picking strategy was this:

- Method A only used downward sweeps.
- Method B only used upward sweeps.
- The remaining picking methods combined sweeps of both directions in various ways.

It should be mentioned that I didn't even list every picking possibility for the licks above. Many times, by forgoing an economy picking opportunity in one instance, you make it possible at a later instance. For instance, in Example 7, you could use Method C for beat 1 (down-up-down-down), but instead of sweeping notes 1 and 2 of beat 2, as in Method C, you use a downstroke for the second note and then use the upward sweep for the third and fourth notes instead. So beat 2 would look like this: up-down-up-up.

The point of these exercises is to help you become aware of the possibilities that exist with this technique. As you may have noted, the stroke direction with which you begin will often dictate whether you're able to sweep up or sweep down at different points in the lick. So, depending on numerous factors (e.g., which feels better to you, what comes before or after, etc.), you can tailor each lick to suit your preference.

If the Economy Is Good, the Country Thrives (And So Does Your Guitar Playing!)

We've been using the term "economy picking" with regard to pick-stroke direction, but there's another side of picking that deals with economy too: *economy of motion*. This is something that's applicable to alternate picking as well. Simply put, the faster you play, the less time you have for your pick to travel from note to note. This means that a lot of wasted motion will prevent you from gaining speed.

You may have noticed a pattern in some of the earlier examples of this chapter. The trouble spots are usually the places where you have to change your pick slant and/or hop over a string. In other words, it's tough if you have to pick, say, a downstroke on string 1, an upstroke on string 2, and another downstroke on string 1. Or if you have to follow an upstroke on string 3 with a downstroke on string 2 and another upstroke on string 3.

To see what I mean, try the following experiment. Play the notes below using both sets of picking directions. Be sure to use a sweeping motion in Method B (and not two separate downstrokes), or you'll defeat the purpose of the experiment!

Play the example slowly and watch your pick hand closely while you do this. You'll most likely find that, with Method B, you're able to maintain your pick angle/slant throughout the phrase. With Method A, though, there will be a slight "bump" in the motion at some point. For most of us who use a bit of a forward pick slant (which is more common than a backward one), this bump will occur before picking the last note. If you're a backward pick-slanter, it will occur before picking the second note. If you hold the pick with no slant at all, you'll probably notice a very slight bump on the second and third note.

Why is this? It's because it's impossible not to. Think about it: after you pick the first note on string 2 with an upstroke, your pick has to travel to the top side of string 3 for the downstroke. If you've started with a forward pick slant, this is no problem, because your pick will be above the plane of the strings and can continue on over string 3. If you've started with a backward pick slant, though, you're in trouble because your pick will be below the plane of the strings and therefore has to come back up to get over string 3—hence the "bump" in motion before the second note.

But don't think I'm only picking on the backward pick-slanters! After picking down on string 3, the forward pick-slanter will now be in trouble because the pick will be below the plane of the strings and will have to hop up to clear string 2—hence the "bump" before the last note. With Method B, however, you can maintain a forward pick slant throughout all three notes because the troublesome string hop has been eliminated.

The problem is, however, that we can't always avoid these awkward string hops if we want to pick every note. If you *do* want to avoid them, you have two options:

1. Move one or more of the notes to a different string, thereby changing the picking layout.

2. Employ some legato moves to remove a troublesome pick stroke.

Guess what? Both of these strategies are commonly employed by both Eric Johnson and Yngwie Malmsteen, which should come as no surprise at this point because they both use a forward pick slant and downward sweeps almost exclusively. For others, though, such as Marshall Harrison and Frank Gambale, who employ upward sweeps as frequently as downward ones, they had to learn how to overcome this trouble area.

That's the purpose of the following exercises: to force these awkward pick moves on you. What you need to focus on is being economical with your pick motions. This basically involves two things:

1. Playing with the very tip of the pick. The farther the tip is buried beneath the plane of the string, the longer it will take to bring it up and over the string.

2. Using small, concise pick strokes. These are not the moments to dig in like Stevie Ray Vaughan.

Pay attention to the picking directions. The thing is, with these exercises, even if you employ one sweep (which is all you will be able to do if picking every note), you're going to end up alternate picking from then on anyway. So there are really only two ways to play them: alternate picking, starting on a downstroke or starting on an upstroke. And, if you employ a sweep, you'll always end up with only one way to pick it. Try it and see!

For instance, in Example 10, you have two spots where you could employ a sweep. You could start with an upstroke and immediately sweep upward from string 2 to string 3. After that, you'd end up with a downstroke for the third note and would therefore have to alternate pick from then on using the picking directions given. Or you could start with an upstroke for the first note and then use a downstroke for the second note, continuing with a downward sweep for the third note. You'd then end up with an upstroke for the fourth note and would have to alternate pick from then on using the picking directions given.

Therefore, the picking directions I've included are the ones that would result after using your one and only available sweep. (Of course, your other option would be to alternate pick it, starting with the opposite direction than what I've shown, but in order to do that repeatedly, you'll be forgoing your opportunity for a sweep, which kind of defeats the purpose of this book!)

Example 10

TRACK 19

Example 11

TRACK 20

Example 12

TRACK 21

Example 13

TRACK 22

JUST BECAUSE YOU CAN…

With regard to my last point about Example 10—about forgoing your opportunity to sweep—I don't want it to sound as though you *should* sweep at every opportunity. Of course, you can do that if you'd prefer, but I'd suggest this simply strategy: do whatever feels better and/or makes it easier on you. If sweeping makes it easier, then do it. After working through this book, you'll be equipped with the skills to do that. But if a sweep doesn't make it easier and/or feel better, then you don't have to use it.

I'll give you an example. Take this stock B minor pentatonic lick:

If you begin with a downstroke, you do have an opportunity for one upward sweep, from string 1 to string 2, which is shown in Method A. From that point on, you'll have to alternate pick it, just as if you'd started with an upstroke, as shown in Method C. However, you can also just alternate pick the whole lick starting with a downstroke, as shown in Method B, choosing to forego that sweep possibility. Since I tend toward slanting my pick forward, this option actually feels best to me, and that's what I do.

So, just because you can sweep, doesn't mean you have to. Once you learn how to do it, it'll be there when you choose to use it (like cruise control on your car), but you don't have to if it doesn't make things easier for you!

Licks

Now let's put your newly polished skills to work with a few more licks. These will be a bit more challenging than those in Chapter 1 and will touch on all the technical concerns we've discussed in this chapter. Pay attention to the picking, and be sure you're playing in time!

This first one is a funky little phrase over an A7 chord that adds some chromatics to an otherwise A Mixolydian line. You can begin with a forward pick slant if you'd like, but by beat 2, move to more of a neutral pick position.

Lick 1

TRACK 23

This one is from the C# minor scale and features three quick sweeps in fairly close proximity. There's also a position shift from ninth to 12th position on beat 3, so be sure not to rush the tempo there. I tend to remain in a neutral pick position throughout this lick.

Lick 2

TRACK 24

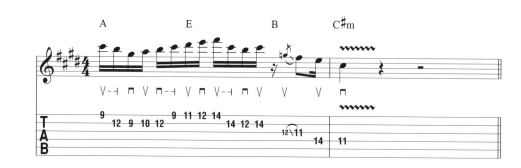

This is a very scalar lick in E minor that also includes position shifts, which allow you to make use of more sweeps. I prefer to shift to 11th position and use my index finger for the last note (F#) of beat 2 in measure 1. In measure 2, I again shift to my index finger for the last note of beat 2, this time located in 14th position. This lick features a nice mixture of downward and upward sweeps throughout. Note also the alternate picking choice for the last three notes. There are two possibilities for a sweep there: down or up. You can choose which one feels better to you.

Lick 3

TRACK 25

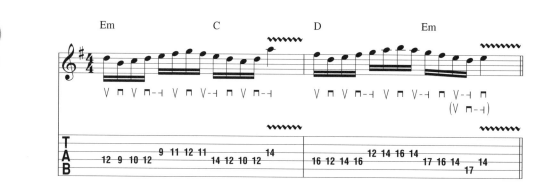

Our final lick of the chapter is a jazzy-sounding line in D minor from the D minor hexatonic scale (D–E–F–G–A–C). In this phrase, we're mixing up some rhythms—16ths and 16th-note triplets—with the sweeps, so take extra care with these to make sure that you're staying in time. Again, note the alternate picking option from beat 1 to beat 2, which allows you to choose between an upward sweep from string 2 to string 3 or a downward sweep from string 4 to string 3.

Lick 4

TRACK 26

At this point, take a bit of a break. You've made it through the "headiest" part of the book. Now that we've got most of the pick-motion analysis out of the way, we'll be able to start progressing more fluidly with the technique, and it should be a bit more fun.

WHAT YOU LEARNED

- Slanting the pick forward or backward can help make the sweeping motion easier when moving in one direction through several strings.

- Economy picking is not "all or nothing." You can choose to employ it at every opportunity or only when you feel it makes things easier.

- There is usually more than one way to employ sweeps during a phrase. You can choose to only sweep with downstrokes, only sweep with upstrokes, or combine both when possible.

- If you forgo a sweeping opportunity at one point in the lick, you'll more than likely have an opportunity to sweep in the opposite direction at a later point.

- Economy of motion (i.e., using the tip of the pick and minimizing pick movements) is critical when you have to make a string hop without using a sweep.

- Just because you *can* sweep, doesn't mean you have to. If a lick (or a portion of one) feels better or makes more sense with alternate picking, feel free to use it.

CHAPTER 3 — THREE-NOTES-PER-STRING SCALES

Often when people think of economy picking, this is what they think of: scales played in groups of three notes on each string. The reason becomes very clear when you try them out: you're able to work your way smoothly across all the strings by using a consistent picking pattern for each string. So why did I not choose to start here? Well, it's been my experience that when people learn economy picking by using three-notes-per-string patterns, they tend to gravitate toward them because it "feels good." Therefore, not only do they end up playing lots of scales straight up and down with the technique, which can get old quite fast, but they also tend to neglect the other facets of the technique, such as moving back and forth quickly between opposing sweeps. In short, three-notes-per-string scales played with economy picking can become a one-trick pony for a lot of players.

However, now that you've already had experience working the technique into other, more musical-sounding examples and licks, developing skills and a deeper understanding of the technique's benefits and shortcomings along the way, I feel you're ready to add this specific skillset to your bag of tricks.

The Basic Idea

It's pretty simple, really. If you continue in one direction while playing a three-notes-per-string pattern, you'll be able to sweep every string cross. Let's take a look at this C major scale pattern that starts in eighth position:

C Major Scale

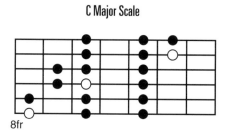

8fr

If you begin on a downstroke and ascend through the scale, you can pick down-up-down for every string, sweeping every time to move to the next string.

Example 1

TRACK 27

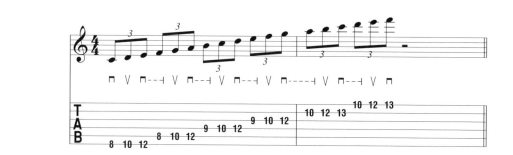

If you begin with an upstroke and descend through the scale, you can pick up-down-up for every string, again sweeping every time you cross strings.

Example 2

TRACK 28

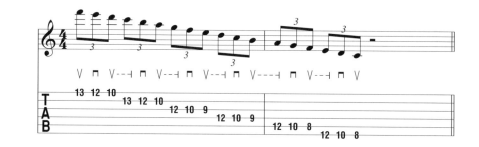

Since you're dealing with three notes on every string, triplets and sextuplets are very common rhythms for obvious reasons. But you can, and definitely should, try playing these in eighth notes, 16th notes, etc. That way, you're able to lock into different rhythms. Try the following examples, making sure that you're steady with your tempo.

Example 3

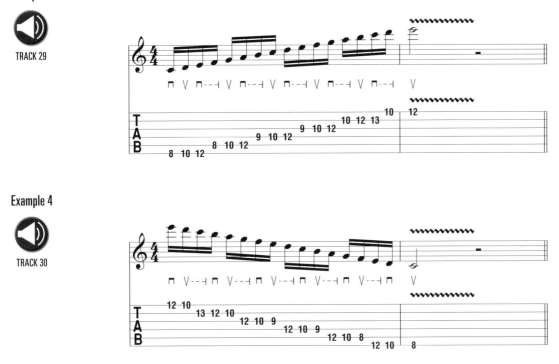

Notice that we started Example 4 with a downstroke. Why? Well, I wanted the lick to resolve to the C note at the end, so that meant I had to start at E. And since there were only two notes on the first string instead of three, I started on a downstroke in order to set up the sweep from string 1 to string 2. From then on, the picking lined up the same way as it did in Example 2.

And this brings us to our next topic…

The Scale Sweeping Formula

If you want to avoid those awkward string hops we talked about in Chapter 2 (e.g., picking a downstroke on string 1 and then an upstroke on string 2) and always use sweeping when you cross a string, there's a formula to which you need to adhere. And it goes like this:

- To keep moving in the same direction, you need an odd number of notes on a string.
- To change direction, you need an even number of notes.

When ascending or descending with three notes on each string, we can see this formula at work: playing three notes (odd number) on every string allows us to sweep at every string change. But what if we want to play up a scale and then come back down? How do we avoid an awkward string hop?

Let's look at the following A minor scale exercise as one possible solution. We're working out of two scale patterns here—one beginning in fifth position and one that begins in seventh position:

A Minor Scale

And here's the exercise:

Example 5

TRACK 31

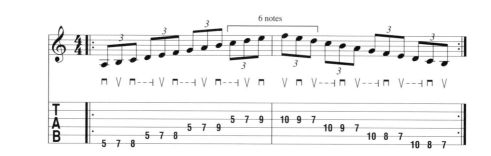

Notice that we have odd numbers of notes (three) on the way up, allowing us to sweep with downstrokes. When we get to string 3, however, we have an even number of notes (six). This turns our picking around and allows us to sweep with upstrokes, continuing with three notes on each string that way as well. As you can see (and hear), you can repeat this pattern ad infinitum, sweeping every time you cross strings.

Of course, it can be any even number; it doesn't have to be six. Below are two more examples that turn around the picking. Example 6, in D minor, uses two notes to do so, and Example 7, in E♭ Mixolydian, uses four notes.

Example 6

TRACK 32

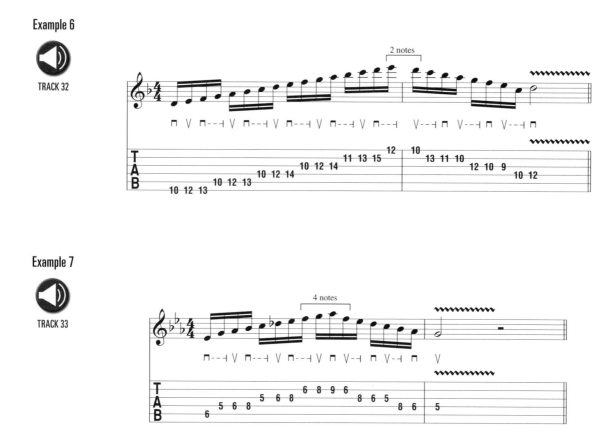

Example 7

TRACK 33

So that's pretty much the idea. As long as you maintain that formula, you can sweep to your heart's desire and never have to endure another string hop as long as you live. Of course, the downside is that playing straight up and down scales like this for an extended period of time will start to lose its luster pretty quick.

This is why it's nice to mix in these three-notes-per-string ideas with some other ideas; it allows you to create phrases that are more musical.

Licks

As mentioned previously, running nothing but scales straight up and down can get a little boring, so in these licks, we're going to mix in a few other ideas with our three-notes-per-string patterns, as this will give us an idea of how these shapes may actually be used in a musical context. In case it's not clear, I've included the three-notes-per-string scale patterns from which each lick is primarily (if not entirely) derived.

This first one is mostly built from the B minor scale and features several changes of direction in the middle of the lick. Note that each one occurs by using an even number of notes: first, two notes on string 2 to start descending, then four notes on string 3 to ascend again, and then two notes on string 2 to start the final descent, during which we add the ♭5th blue note (F♮).

Lick 1

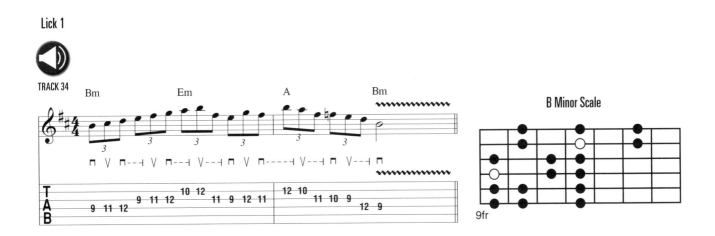

This one is based out of G Dorian and begins with an ascent of strings 2 and 1 in eighth position. We then shift up to 10th position for the descent, using six notes on string 1 to turn us around. After that, it's three notes per string all the way down. Notice, though, that we're not just playing scales the whole time.

Lick 2

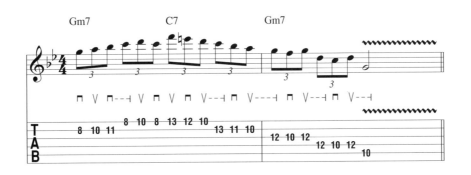

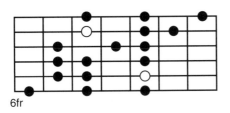

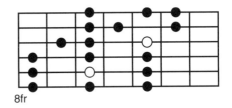

Here's a line from C Mixolydian with a few chromatics thrown in for color. Again, we're using odd numbers of notes to continue moving in one direction and even numbers to change direction. After using three notes each on strings 5 and 4, for example, we use five notes on string 3. Since it's an odd number, though, we can continue sweeping with downstrokes. We use two notes on string 1 to change direction, three notes on string 2 to keep descending, and then four notes on string 3 to change direction once again, this time for the final C note.

Lick 3

TRACK 36

C Mixolydian Mode

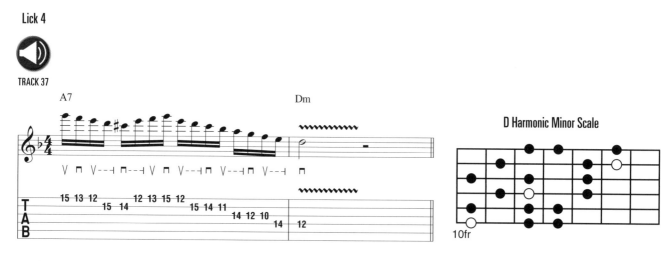

6fr

This one uses the D harmonic minor scale and features several direction changes at the beginning before it settles into the final descent. I recommend keeping the pick in a neutral position for the first three beats.

Lick 4

TRACK 37

Again, I've tried to demonstrate with these licks that, just because you're playing within three-notes-per-string patterns, you can do more than simply run straight up or down the scales. I think it's important to practice with this in mind because, as it's often said, "We tend to play what we practice."

WHAT YOU LEARNED

- By organizing scales in patterns of three notes on every string, we can ascend or descend straight through them while using a sweep for every string cross: down-up-down, down-up-down when ascending, and up-down-up, up-down-up when descending.

- These patterns can become a crutch for some players, as they tend to rely on them excessively. That's why it's always nice to mix other ideas into these patterns so they don't become too predictable.

- If you want to sweep every string cross, remember the sweeping formula: an odd number of notes per string when you want to keep going in the same direction, and an even number of notes when you want to change direction.

SECTION 2: SPECIFIC APPLICATIONS
CHAPTER 4 – REPETITIVE THREE-NOTE PATTERNS

In this chapter, we'll explore some nifty little tricks with three-note groupings that economy picking makes possible. These would be very difficult to pull off with strict alternate picking, yet they can be mastered fairly quickly with the economy technique. Like the three-notes-per-string scales, you don't want to overdo these kinds of things, but they do have their place. Just ask Yngwie!

Triad Arpeggios

In case you don't know, a triad is a chord containing three different notes: a root (the note that gives the chord its name), a 3rd, and a 5th. The four main types are *major* (1–3–5), *minor* (1–♭3–5), *augmented* (1–3–♯5), and *diminished* (1–♭3–♭5). Because they span a good amount of ground, they can be troublesome for the alternate picker. Economy picking, however, handles them pretty well.

Let's start out with a simple C major triad on strings 6 and 5. Here's the shape:

C Major Triad

7fr

If you repeat these notes as a triplet figure, there are two possibilities for a sweep: a downstroke sweep or an upstroke sweep.

If you're saying, "Wait! You missed an opportunity to sweep in Method A!" you're correct. You could also sweep with an upstroke from the last note of beat 1 to the first note in beat 2. However, if you do that, then you'll have switched to Method B for the duration of the lick, so there's not really a point to it.

So you can choose which method feels better to you. To me, Method A feels much better, and it's no coincidence why: I'm a forward pick-slanter, and this allows me to maintain that slant throughout the lick. This is also the way Yngwie would play arpeggios like this. With Method B, it's more troublesome for me to hop over string 6 after picking it with an upstroke. But you should try both methods to see which feels best to you.

To really get a feel for this idea, try this next little exercise, which moves the same arpeggio pattern around.

Example 1

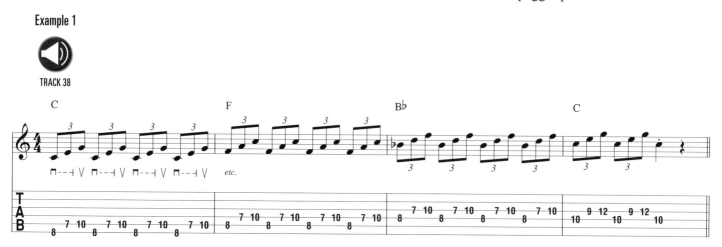

TRACK 38

Of course, by using the other triad shapes, we can get a little more harmonically adventurous. Here are all the shapes on the different string groups for reference (if you don't know them already).

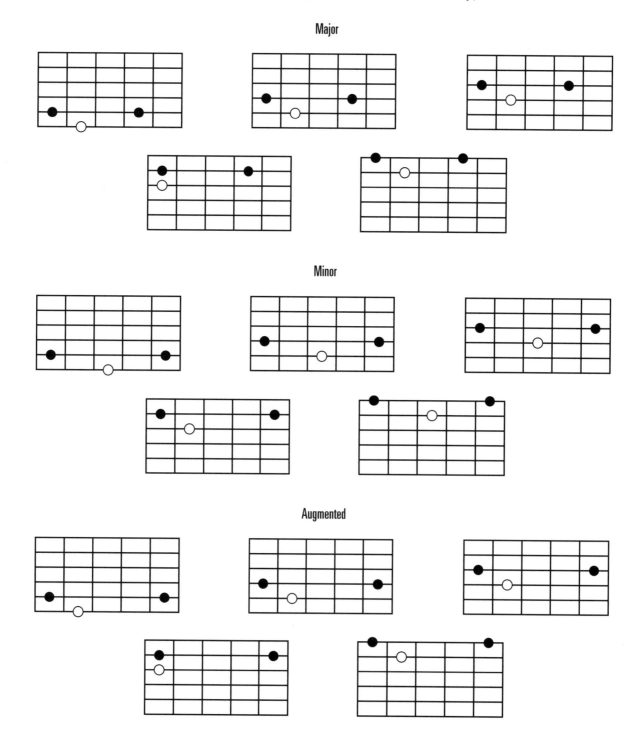

Diminished

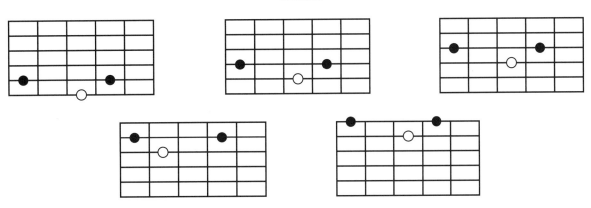

And now let's make use of some of these shapes in a few more exercises.

Example 2

TRACK 39

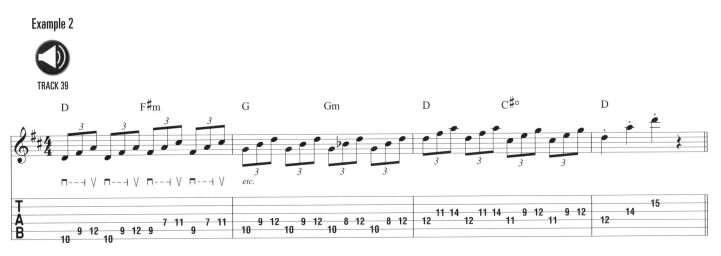

This next example makes use of the shapes on strings 3 and 2, which are a little different than the others.

Example 3

TRACK 40

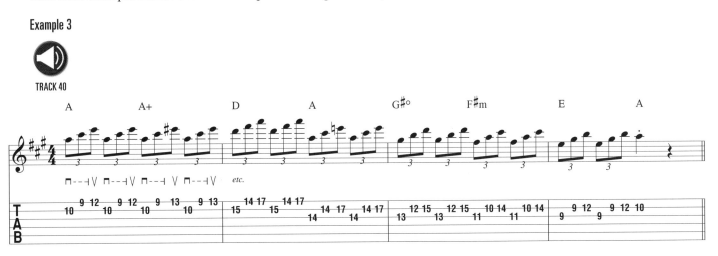

Of course, you don't have to use triplets and you can play the notes in a different order as well. As long as the shape is the same (two notes on one string and one on the next) and you're playing them in groups of three, you can use the same picking pattern. There may be times when you need to add a sweep when changing direction, but then you can get back to the same pattern. The next example demonstrates this. Notice how we add one upstroke sweep at the end of measure 1 to right the ship for measure 2.

Example 4

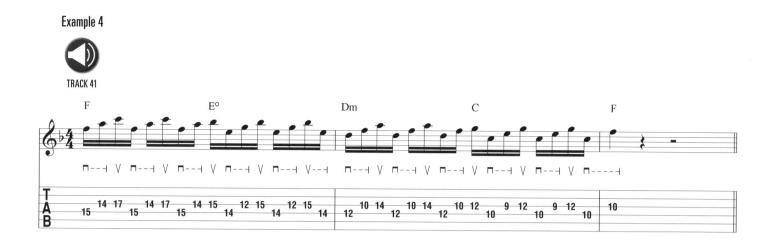

Here's an exercise specifically geared toward "righting the ship" by throwing in one necessary upward sweep while switching to another string group. Watch the picking directions closely, especially at the end of each measure.

Example 5

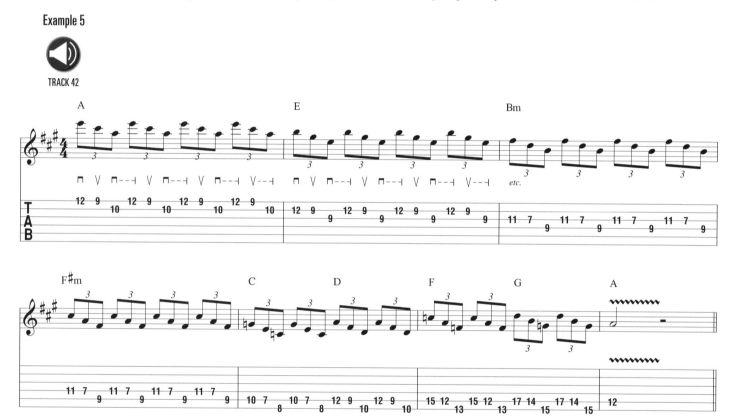

When you're moving more than one string set, as when playing the same arpeggio in different octaves, for instance, it gets a little trickier. Ascending is still pretty easy because you can maintain a forward pick slant throughout. Descending, though, isn't as tidy. After the upward sweep at the end of beats 2 and 4 in measure 3, you'll have to hop over a string before picking down again. And that can take a little practice.

Example 6

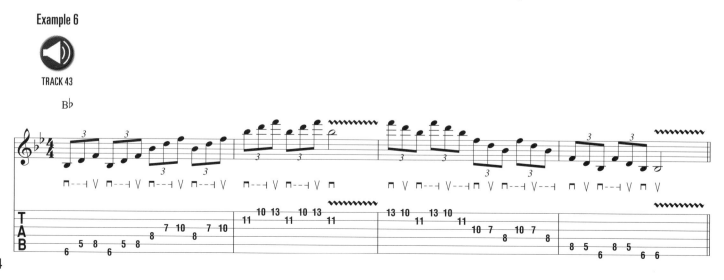

Other Three-Note Groupings

Besides arpeggios, we can use this same technique for other three-note groups as well. The pentatonic scale is a prime example. For instance, here's how we can create a three-note sequence within the A minor pentatonic scale. Note that we're using the exact same picking pattern as with the triad arpeggios.

Example 7

Here's another idea using the A minor pentatonic scale. We're playing a more intervallic-sounding pattern with 4ths and just moving that up to each position of the scale. We slightly alter the note pattern at the very end in order to make the line resolve better, but this is the same picking pattern.

Example 8

Again, this is the way that's easiest for me to pick these phrases, but as I mentioned before, you can choose to use an upstroke sweep as well if it's easier for you. For instance, Example 8 could also be picked: down-up-up, down-up-up, etc.

In fact, when you turn this pattern on its head, and you have two notes on the lower-pitched string and one on the higher, I do prefer to use upstroke sweeps, along with a backward pick slant. Here's an example of that idea:

Example 9

Again, you could choose to pick that example as up-down-down, up-down-down, etc. I encourage you to try both to see what feels best. You can't have it both ways, but one will likely feel better than the other.

Licks

Now let's hear these ideas applied to some different licks. Lick 1 begins by revving up with a three-note A major scale fragment. After four repetitions, it launches into ascending arpeggios (A and G) before resolving to the major 3rd of A (C♯), followed by the tonic (A). Since we have two notes on the lower-pitched string and one on the higher on beats 1–2, I'm using a backward pick slant with upstroke sweeps. If you wanted to make this lick work with all downstroke sweeps, you could move the B note at fret 9 of string 4 to fret 4 of string 3.

Lick 1

TRACK 47

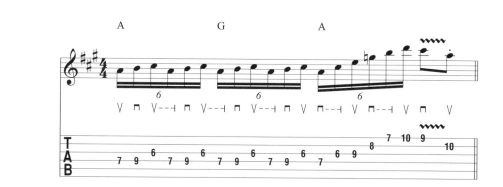

We're playing 16th-note rhythms in this next lick, using a specific rhythmic formula for each measure: two groups of three notes and one group of two notes. This creates a syncopated 16th-note phrase that equals two beats. After spending measures 1 and 2 entirely on the top two strings, we begin descending through the strings in measure 3. I've added fret-hand fingerings here to help with the shifts. This is the one part where we'll need to throw in a couple of upstroke sweeps, just as we did in Example 6.

Lick 2

TRACK 48

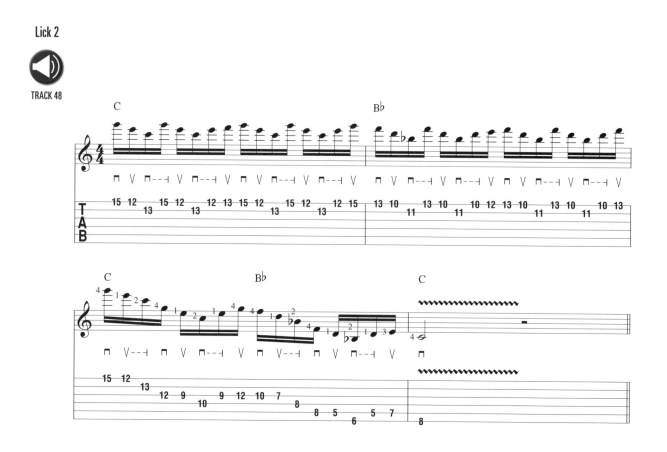

This one is rhythmically similar to Lick 2, in that we're repeating three-note groups in a 16th-note rhythm to get a syncopated feel. In this lick, however, we're playing five groups of three notes and adding one note at the end to round out the phrase. In other words, it's 15 + 1, which equals one measure of 16th notes. Watch for the two upward sweeps: one at the end of each measure.

Lick 3

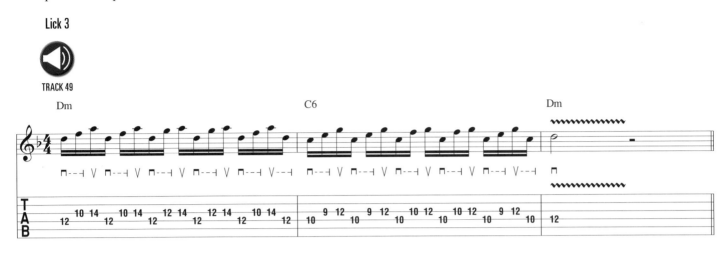

The final lick in this chapter is one of the most challenging thus far in the book due to the prevalence of sweeps—downward and upward—throughout. The basic idea is that we're alternating an ascending arpeggio with a descending scale fragment. The picking pattern for most of the lick will be down-down-up, down-up-up. You'll get some practice rolling your index finger from string 3 to string 2 here with the Eb and F chords. Try to make them two separate notes instead of holding it down like a barre.

Lick 4

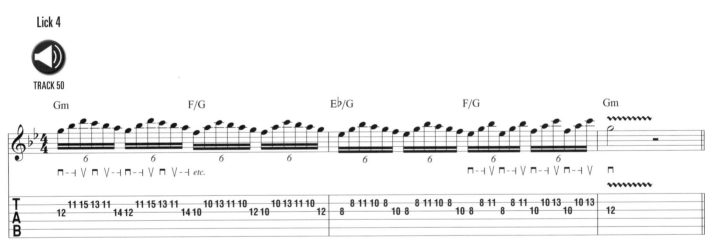

WHAT YOU LEARNED

- A *triad* is a three-note chord consisting of a root, a 3rd, and a 5th.

- The four common triads are *major* (1–3–5), *minor* (1–b3–5), *augmented* (1–3–#5), and *diminished* (1–b3–b5).

- When playing a triad arpeggio as a two-string shape, you can choose to sweep up or down.

- Just because they have three notes doesn't mean you have to play them in a triplet rhythm. When played as 16th notes, triads create syncopation.

- When switching to a new string group, it's sometimes necessary to throw in an extra sweep to "right the ship" for the picking hand.

- You can apply the three-note grouping idea to scales as well, including the pentatonic scale.

CHAPTER 5 – REPETITIVE FOUR-NOTE PATTERNS

Just as we did with three-note groupings in Chapter 4, we can apply economy picking to certain four-note groupings in creative ways. The main difference here is that, with the three-note groupings, you could choose whether you wanted to use downward sweeps or upward ones. With these four-note groupings, you'll be using both consistently. Let's see how this is done.

Pentatonic Ideas

One common application for this type of thing is four-note pentatonic sequences. Here's an example in A minor pentatonic:

Most people would likely pick this lick (assuming they're not using any legato) with alternate picking, and this is certainly a fine way to do it. It allows you to maintain a forward pick slant, so it's possible to generate a lot of speed doing it. Eric Johnson can attest to that fact, as he uses alternate picking for this type of lick.

But you can also play it with sweep picking: simply alternate down- and up-sweeps for an endless loop.

Example 1

TRACK 51

For this idea, I find that using a neutral pick position, as opposed to alternating forward and backward pick slants, works best for me. It'll take a bit of practice to get used to the timing. It's easy to sound lopsided at first, but once you get it, it really feels effortless for the pick hand. One good exercise for this is to simply mute the strings with your fret hand, focusing solely on the picking motion. That will help to identify any problem areas (if there are any).

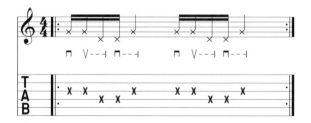

As long as you stay on the same two strings, you can move the sequence anywhere. Here we run up through every position of A minor pentatonic:

Example 2

Here's an example in G minor pentatonic in which we're climbing up each position while alternating ascending and descending four-note sequences. So we've essentially added two notes for a total of four on each string. But since it's an even number, we can still alternate down- and up-sweeps the same way.

Example 3

However, if you move to a different string set (e.g., if you want to run a four-note sequence across the strings instead of down the neck), you can do that, but you'll lose the ability to sweep every other sequence. For example, here's an idea in A minor pentatonic in which we play two four-note groups on each string set. Notice that, after the initial set of two groupings, which are just like the previous examples, we're not able to sweep the first four-note grouping on each new string set. So, starting from beat 3, the recurring pattern is: down-up-down-up, up-down-down-up. The good thing is that you don't have any awkward string hops for the picking hand; the tradeoff is that you have back-and-forth shifts for the fret hand.

Example 4

As an alternative to the previous example, on the following page is another way you could play the same exercise. This one will stay in one position for the fret hand, but you'll have a little more awkwardness in the pick hand. There are two ways to play this one. With Method A, you forgo one sweep, but you can maintain your forward slant throughout the lick, save for the very last note of beats 2 and 4. With Method B, you sweep at every opportunity, but you have one extra string hop, which occurs on the second note of beats 2 and 4. Method A works better for me, but try them both out to see which feels best.

Example 5

TRACK 55

Seventh-Note Arpeggios

A seventh chord adds one note, the 7th, on top of a triad, so it has four notes: a root, 3rd, 5th, and 7th. There are five common seventh chords:

- Major Seventh (maj7): 1–3–5–7
- Minor Seventh (m7): 1–♭3–5–♭7
- Dominant Seventh (7): 1–3–5–♭7
- Minor Seventh Flat-Five, also called "half diminished" (m7♭5): 1–♭3–♭5–♭7
- Diminished Seventh, also called "fully diminished" (°7): 1–♭3–♭5–♭♭7 (6)

There are others possibilities as well, but we won't look at them here. Below are some usable patterns for playing these arpeggios on two-string groups. The root of each shape is an open circle.

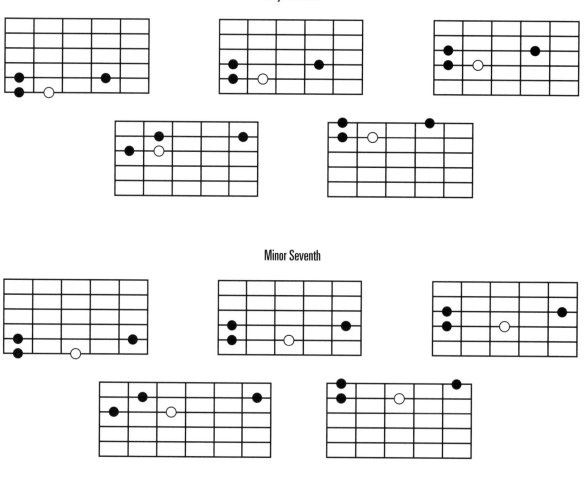

Major Seventh

Minor Seventh

Dominant Seventh

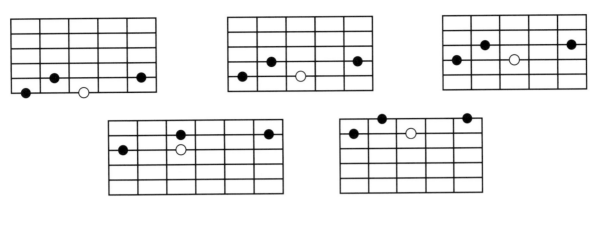

Minor Seventh Flat-Five

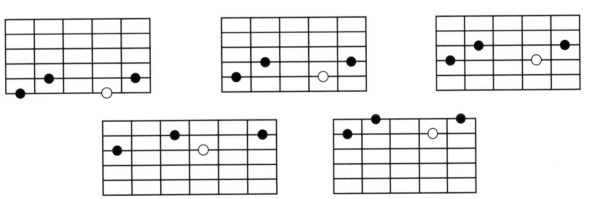

Diminished Seventh

So, as you may have suspected, we can apply the same picking techniques to these shapes as we did to our pentatonic ones.

Example 6

TRACK 56

Example 7

TRACK 57

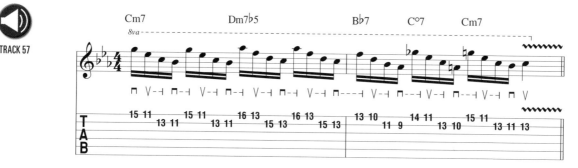

The shapes given above all had the 7th degree as the lowest note, which puts the chords in third inversion, but you can use other inversions as well. Shapes with the 3rd (first inversion) or 5th (second inversion) on the bottom usually work well. The root on the bottom is usually a bit too stretchy, however.

Making use of more than one inversion provides for smoother voice leading. This example mixes a first-inversion A♭maj7 chord, a third-inversion D♭maj7 chord, and a second-inversion E♭7 chord:

Example 8

TRACK 58

And again, if we double the amount of notes on either string, we can still maintain the sweeps. Here's an example of that in E♭ with a triplet rhythm, using four notes on string 4 and two notes on string 3. We're using a second-inversion E♭maj7, a third-inversion D♭maj7, and a third-inversion E♭maj7.

Example 9

TRACK 59

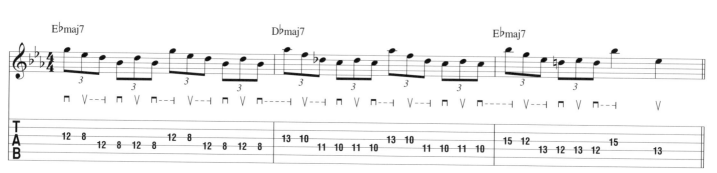

Licks

Now let's check out these ideas with some licks. This first one is in F major and takes place entirely on strings 4 and 3, so the picking is totally straightforward. We begin with F major pentatonic in measure 1, changing only the top note on beat 3 to imply D minor pentatonic. In measure 2, we play an Am7 arpeggio in third inversion (with the ♭7th, G, as the lowest note), which creates a C6 sound over the C chord, before ending with an E note bent a half step up to the tonic, F.

Lick 1

TRACK 60

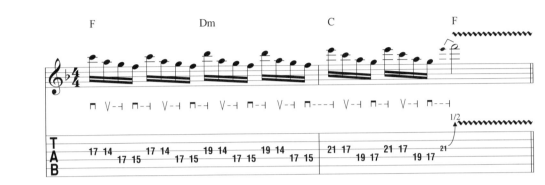

Here's an arpeggio workout on the top two strings in the key of A. Aside from beats 3–4 of measure 1, which is a maj7♯5 arpeggio, all of these shapes should be familiar. One difference here from the examples earlier in the chapter is that we're beginning with the sweep right away instead of playing two notes on the same string first. So the pattern is shifted over one note, but the picking technique of sweeping two notes in opposite directions throughout is still the same. This is done to help show some of the possibilities that exist with these ideas.

Lick 2

TRACK 61

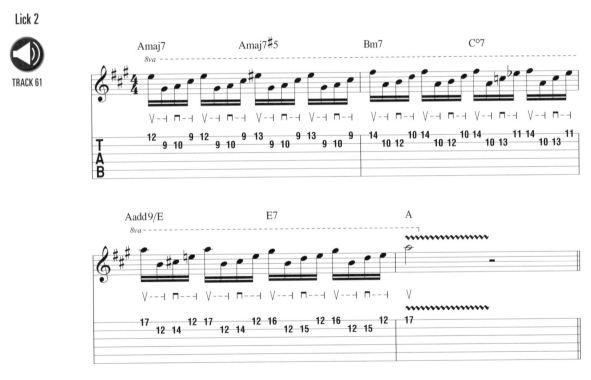

Following is a fusion-type line that makes use of a concept from Example 9: doubling the number of notes on one string. In this case, we're playing four notes on string 3 and two notes on string 4 for most of the measure. But since we're playing these as 16th notes, after twice through the six-note sequence, we still have four 16th notes left in the measure. Therefore, we remove two notes from string 3 and just play two on string 3 and two on string 4 to round out the measure. We're playing over an altered dominant chord (A13♭9) here, and the scale we're using is called the *half-whole diminished scale*. It's an eight-note scale of alternating half and whole steps and is a great choice for playing over an altered dominant with a ♭9th and a natural 13th. The A half-whole diminished is spelled: A–B♭–C–C♯–D♯–E–F♯–G. What's interesting about this scale is that it's symmetrical. You can move a pattern up or down in minor 3rds and you'll still be playing the scale, just starting from a different note. So be sure to notice that measures 2 and 3 are the exact same fingering as measure 1, only in a different spot on the neck. In measure 4, the tension is released by resolving to a D minor chord.

43

Lick 3

This lick is a more inside-sounding variation on the technique used in Lick 3. We're playing the same syncopated six-against-four rhythmic idea, but instead of moving laterally along the neck, we've moving across it to different string groups. The scale used here is C Dorian, and we're mostly based in eighth position. At the very end, we shift up to 10th position to resolve the line.

Lick 4

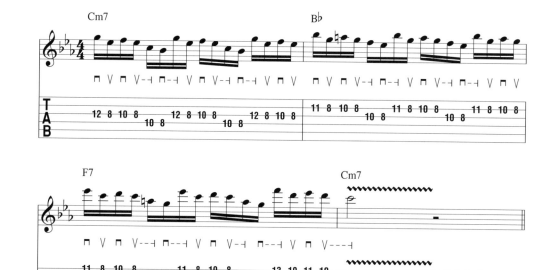

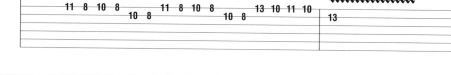

WHAT YOU LEARNED

- When playing a four-note group in which you're alternating two notes on adjacent strings, you can use alternating sweeps every time you cross strings.

- You can double the notes (to four) on either or both strings and still use the same alternating sweep technique for each string change.

- A *seventh chord* is a four-note chord with a root, 3rd, 5th, and 7th. The most common seventh chords are *major seventh* (1–3–5–7), *minor seventh* (1–♭3–5–♭7), *dominant seventh* (1–3–5–♭7), *minor seventh flat-five* (1–♭3–♭5–♭7), and *diminished seventh* (1–♭3–♭5–♭7).

- Seventh chord arpeggios can usually be comfortably arranged as two-string patterns in first inversion (3rd on the bottom), second inversion (5th on the bottom), or third inversion (7th on the bottom), but root position requires very large stretches (especially if low on the neck).

CHAPTER 6 – ADDING LEGATO

So far, all the examples in this book have had one thing in common: every single note is picked. This is, of course, hardly the case with real music, but it's been necessary in order to learn the technique of economy picking. In this chapter, we're finally going to give our picking hand a bit of relief by learning how we can mix legato and economy picking techniques.

The Forward Pick-Slanting Cheat

I won't spend too much time on this because it's not really economy picking, but I just wanted to mention how players like Yngwie Malmsteem get around having to pick awkward things when descending. As mentioned before, Yngwie will employ downstroke sweeps when ascending through a scale with three notes per string. But his forward pick-slant makes it difficult to use an upward sweep, so he doesn't use economy picking when descending through a three-notes-per-string scale. Instead, he uses a pull-off to make it more manageable for the pick hand.

Here's a typical example in E minor to demonstrate how this might work:

Example 1

TRACK 64

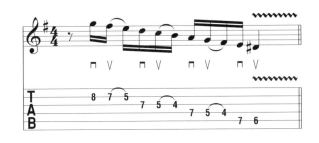

As you can see, he never has to follow a downstroke on a higher-pitched string with an upstroke on the adjacent lower-pitched string, which is a troublesome move if you use a forward pick-slant exclusively. Of course, this rule only applies when he's playing at hyper speed. At slower speeds, he may break this rule if necessary.

If a phrase has four notes on some strings, such as the harmonic minor phrase below, he can pick more notes if he wants to, but he'll still use strategically placed pull-offs to avoid that awkward pick stroke that he doesn't like.

Example 2

TRACK 65

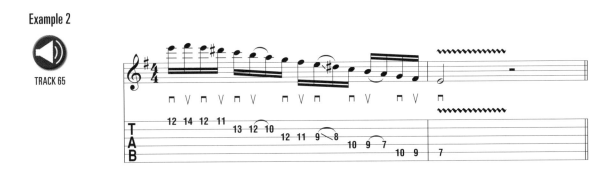

So, in other words, as long as he's moving to a lower string after an upstroke or after a legato note (slide, pull-off, or hammer-on), he's happy. Of course, Yngwie is not the only person who uses this idea. You can do the same thing, and it doesn't have to be with the harmonic minor scale either!

Here's an example in B Dorian in which we employ some downstroke sweeps among the series of pull-off "cheats."

Example 3

So the basic idea is to simply employ a legato move to save you from an awkward pick stroke.

Scale Sequences

Let's take a more structured look at this idea using a three-notes-per-string scale pattern to play a descending four-note sequence. We'll work from this E major scale form:

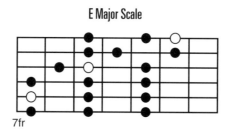

E Major Scale

7fr

Now, if we had to play this sequence as a forward pick-slanter would, we'll need to employ some pull-offs in order to avoid awkward pick moves.

Example 4

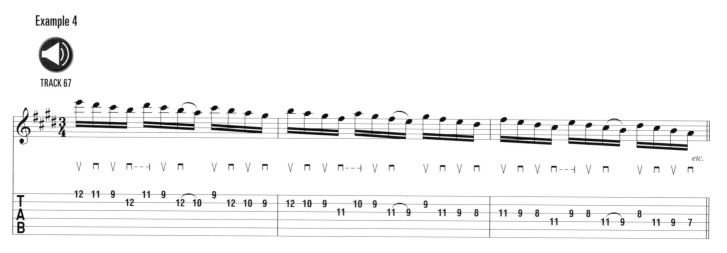

So, we can see that there's a three-beat pattern that repeats:
- Up-down-up-down
- Down-up-down-pull
- Up-down-up-down

After that, it starts all over again with up-down-up-down in measure 2. (Of course, you don't have to play this sequence in 3/4, but it makes the pattern easier to see.) Again, this is applicable to the forward pick-slanter who only prefers to sweep with downstrokes.

If you're not afraid of upstroke sweeps, there are several other ways to skin the cat. First, let's look at how we could employ economy picking if we wanted to pick every note.

Example 5

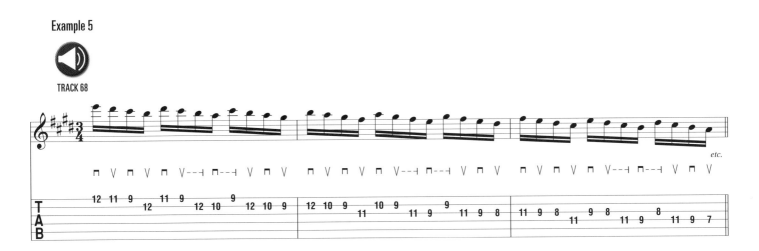

TRACK 68

So, the three-beat pattern here is as follows:
- Down-up-down-up
- Down-up-up-down
- Down-up-down-up

So we get two sweeps for each three-beat pattern. By the way, if you're wondering why I didn't begin with an upstroke for the very first note, which would allow for an upward sweep from string 1 to string 2, good catch! The reason I didn't do that is because that option is only good for that spot. Once the three-beat pattern repeats, you'll always be starting on a downstroke (as in the first notes of measures 2 and 3). This way, I was able to show how the pattern actually repeats each time.

One way we could make this easier on the pick hand is by using a pull-off during the first beat of each three-beat pattern. This would also allow us to add one downward sweep.

Example 6

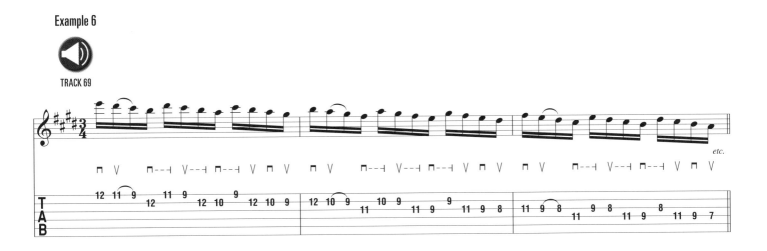

TRACK 69

So, the three-beat pattern is:
- Down-up-pull-down
- Down-up-up-down
- Down-up-down-up

This helps for sure, but we still have the awkward moment at the beginning of beat 3 in each measure, where we have to pick down on string 1 and then up on string 2. By adding one more pull-off, we can get rid of that problem and still maintain the same number of sweeps.

Example 7

TRACK 70

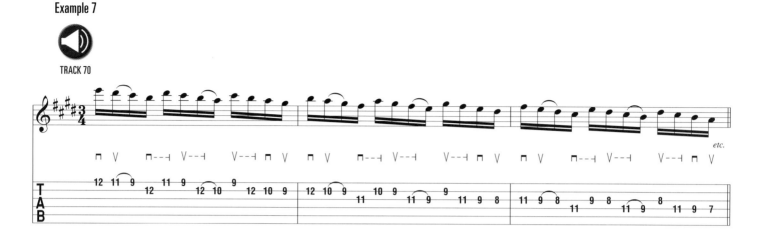

This makes the three-beat pattern:
- Down-up-pull-down
- Down-up-up-pull
- Up-up-down-up

So, we have two upstroke sweeps in a row from beat 2 to beat 3, but the pull-off between them gives you plenty of time to make it happen.

Having tried each variation on this sequence (i.e., Examples 4–7), which do you prefer? They all have their advantages, and it really only comes down to personal preference.

Other Applications

Another way we can employ legato is with repetitive triplet (or sextuplet) licks that alternate three notes on two strings. For example, take this repetitive phrase:

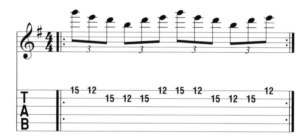

Since there are three notes on each string, and we're changing directions each time, there's no way to incorporate a sweep when repeating this lick. You could get one sweep in the first time you played it, but then you'd have to resort to strict alternate picking for every repeat thereafter. (Try it if you don't believe me!)

However, by adding a legato note, you can use a sweep during every repetition. There are two different choices, depending on whether you want to sweep down or up. Here is the first choice...

Example 8A

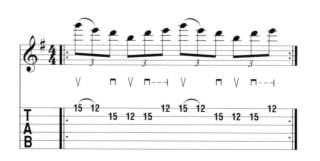

TRACK 71

And here is the second...

Example 8B

Here's another take on the four-note descending scale sequence. With this method, we're remaining on the same two strings and shifting down after one repetition of the picking pattern—in this case, every two beats. We're using the E Dorian mode here.

Example 9

TRACK 73

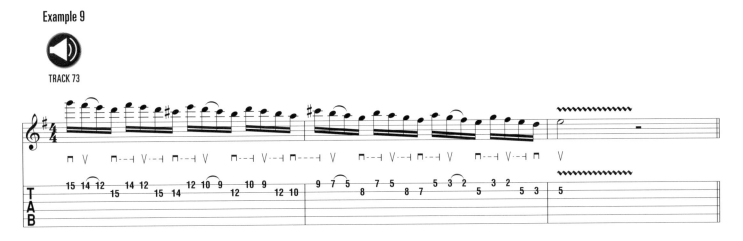

So, the two-beat picking pattern is:
- Down-up-pull-down
- Down-up-up-down

This means we have three sweeps for every two beats, which is not bad at all. The fret-hand shifts will take a bit of practice, but they're doable.

You can also apply a legato move to our triad arpeggios. Here's an example of that in D using D, F♯, G, and A arpeggios. Four downward sweeps, and you're out!

Example 10

TRACK 74

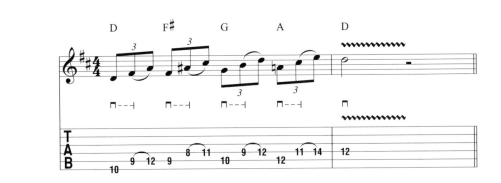

Legato is a great way to lessen the burden on your picking hand when you come across something that's really giving you problems. The good news is that it often ends up sounding just as good as, if not better than, the all-picked option. There are really no limits to how you can apply these ideas.

Licks

Our first lick is a variation of the phrase in Example 3. This one only includes downward sweeps, so it would be best suited for exclusive forward pick-slanters.

Lick 1

TRACK 75

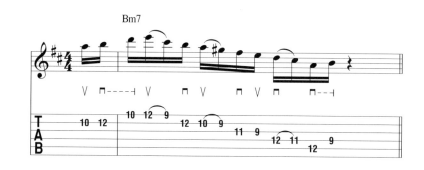

Here's a line in A Dorian that accentuates the 9th (B) of the Am9 chord. Again, there's more than one way to pick this line. For example, if I hadn't used a hammer-on on beat 1, I could have picked down-up-down and then swept down to the note on string 3. But that would have resulted in an awkward movement of having to pick down on string 3 (last note of beat 1) and then up on string 4 (first note of beat 2). By using the hammer-on, I'm allowed to sweep upward at that point instead. Notice that the same two-beat picking pattern is repeated again on beats 3 and 4.

Lick 2

TRACK 76

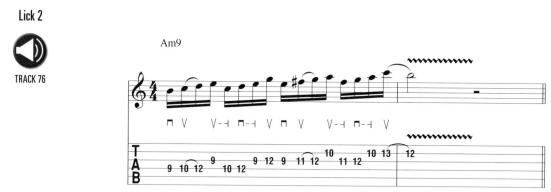

This lick, played over a Cm7 chord, makes use of the C blues scale in the home base of eighth position. It's a great example of mixing sweeps and pull-offs throughout to facilitate smooth articulation that's relatively problem-free for the pick hand. Every pull-off has its purpose, whether it's to immediately avoid an awkward pick stroke or to set up a subsequent sweep.

Lick 3

TRACK 77

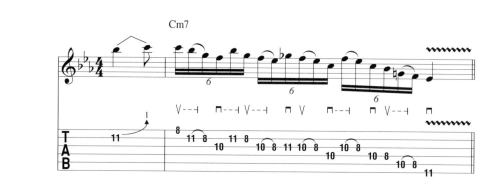

This last lick combines F♯ minor hexatonic (F♯–G♯–A–B–C♯–E) and the F♯ blues scale. We make use of a lot of sweeps throughout, but again, the legato moves help to avoid some trouble spots.

Lick 4

TRACK 78

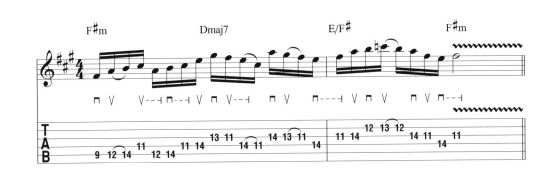

WHAT YOU LEARNED

- If you're strictly a forward pick-slanter, you can use pull-offs when descending a three-notes-per-string scale to avoid awkward pick strokes. The pattern for each string would be: down-up-pull, down-up-pull, etc.

- In a descending four-note scale sequence, there are several options for employing pull-offs (or hammer-ons if ascending) to help ease the burden on the picking hand. You should experiment with each to see which feels best to you. When playing this type of sequence in 16th notes, with a three-notes-per-string pattern, your picking pattern will repeat after every three beats.

- You can add one legato move to a repeating lick in which there are an odd number of notes—such as three—on each of two adjacent strings. The spot you choose will determine whether you're able to use a downward or upward sweep.

- There are innumerable ways you can combine legato moves with economy picking; you just have to experiment when necessary.

CHAPTER 7 – EXTENDED SWEEP PICKING

Although sometimes the terms "economy picking" and "sweep picking" are used interchangeably—I've been saying "sweep" a lot, for sure—I'm going to refer to anything beyond a two-string sweep as *extended sweep picking* (or just "sweep picking" for short). This means you'll be sweeping three, four, five, or six strings in a row.

Interestingly, many players who otherwise don't use the economy picking technique for scales will use the extended sweep technique quite often. The reason for this is quite plain: there's just no easier way to play large arpeggios. Although some players, such as Steve Morse and Martin Miller (if you haven't checked him out on YouTube, do so now!), can blow through arpeggios at very impressive speeds by using alternate picking, it's still simply no contest compared to sweep picking. With sweep picking, the only practical speed limit is that of your fretting hand.

Three-String Sweeps

Let's start with three-string sweeps, which are probably the most common. Even some players who don't engage in sweeping gymnastics will often employ a three-string sweep amidst their scalar playing. Eric Johnson is a prime example. You're not going to see him sweeping up and down five or six strings like Michael Angelo Batio, but he'll use an ascending three-string sweep quite frequently in his pentatonic runs.

The classic application of the three-string sweep is the triad arpeggio in root position, first inversion, or second inversion. In case you're not familiar with all these shapes, let's quickly take a look at them on various string groups in major and minor form.

Major-Root Position

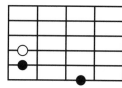 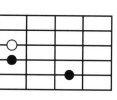 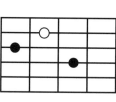 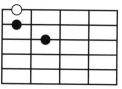

Major-First Inversion

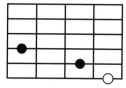 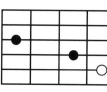

Major-Second Inversion

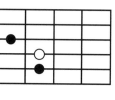 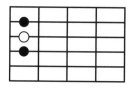 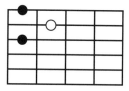

Minor-Root Position

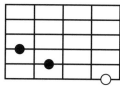 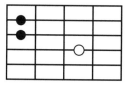

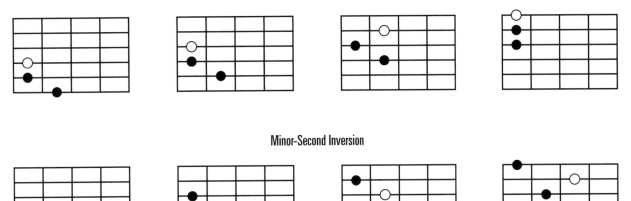

Minor-First Inversion

Minor-Second Inversion

(**Note:** We'll make use of more extended arpeggio shapes in this chapter as well. If any of them are new to you, check out the Appendix to see them all laid out.)

Often, these shapes are swept in ascending fashion, and a note is added on the top string—often an octave higher than the lowest note—to create a triplet/sextuplet phrase. Try the following exercises slowly at first to make sure you're not rushing or dragging through the sweeps. Notice that we add a pull-off at the top to set up the next round of sweeps. We're only sweeping with downstrokes here.

Example 1

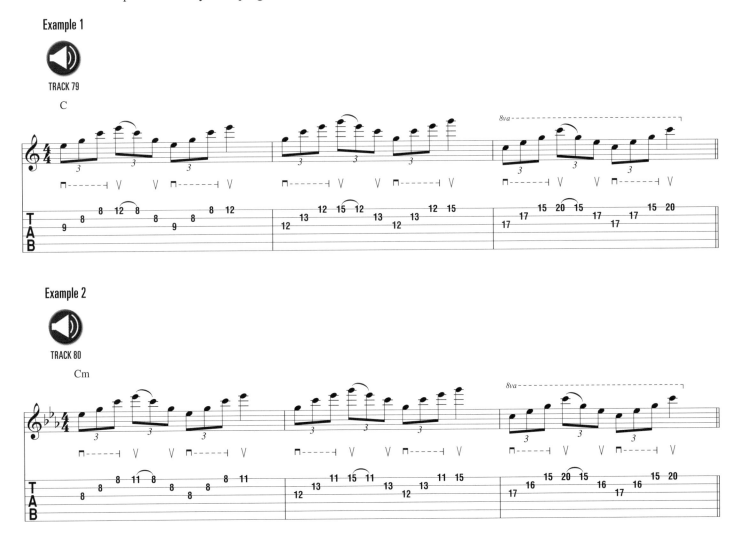

TRACK 79

Example 2

TRACK 80

You'll notice that, if you try to play some of these too low on the neck, there are some pretty fierce stretches involved. For example, if you were to transpose measure 3 of Examples 1 and 2 down an octave, to third position, you'd have to pull off from fret 8 to fret 3. This may be simply out of the question for some people. So these types of things will determine which shapes are most commonly used and where.

Other string groups may be different in this regard. For instance, whereas the first-inversion major form—measure 1 in the previous Example 1—is doable at fairly low spots on the neck with the 3–1 string group, when you move it to the 4–2 string group, it's much less manageable.

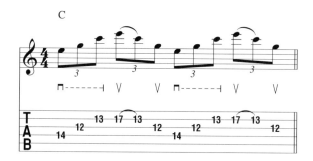

This is, of course, because you have to fret the first note on string 2 with your middle finger, which will seriously limit your stretching ability. You may be able to squeak it out here in 12th position, but if you move it down even three frets, to an A arpeggio, it will start to get pretty hairy for most people.

So this is all to say that not all of the shapes are as usable as others at times; it depends on what you're trying to do.

Now let's try a few triad arpeggio exercises that show how these shapes are typically used. The first one here is in A minor. One of the most difficult shapes to play cleanly occurs in measure 2: the first-inversion minor form on strings 3–1 (in this case, Dm). You have to roll your index finger over three strings in order to keep the notes separate, which is not easy to do.

Example 3

TRACK 81

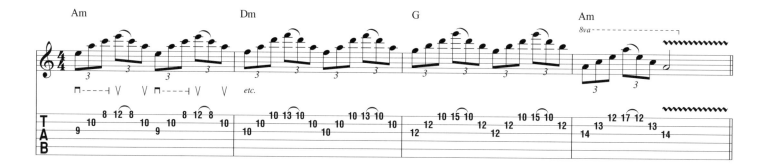

And here's one in G major that demonstrates a few other possibilities. First of all, we're starting at the top and descending first. And secondly, you can use other rhythms besides triplets, so we're using 16th notes here. This creates a six-against-four *hemiola*, as the pattern is six notes long. Because of this, after two times through the pattern, we have one beat (four 16th notes) left over, so we fill it in with just a descent. Also note that at the end of measure 2, we go ahead and use an upward sweep for the last two notes of the C major arpeggio since we don't have to prepare for another downward sweep.

Example 4

TRACK 82

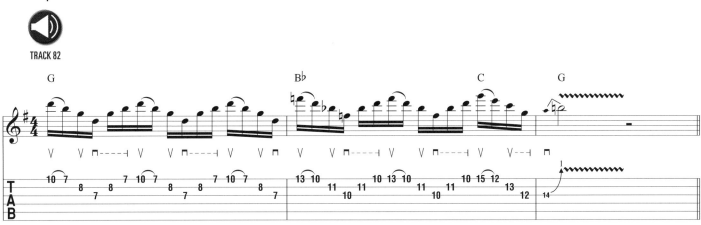

Although it's not as common, you can also up-sweep through these shapes. This exercise in B minor demonstrates this with four-note groupings of 16th notes. The picking pattern is down-up-up-up for every beat. The hardest part here is moving from the upstroke on string 3 to the downstroke on string 1. You'll need to transfer to a forward pick slant as you strike the notes on string 3 each time. But it can be done.

Example 5

TRACK 83

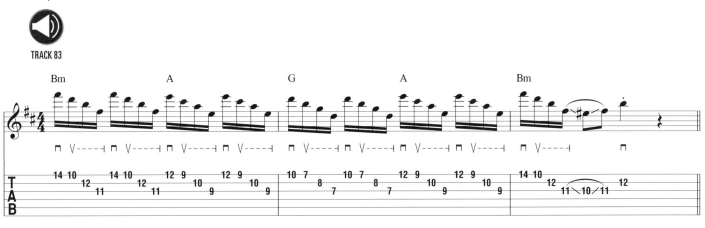

This next example ups the ante. We're playing sextuplets here by way of adding two notes on the top string. The picking is the same as in Example 5, just with an added down-up at the beginning of each beat.

Example 6

TRACK 84

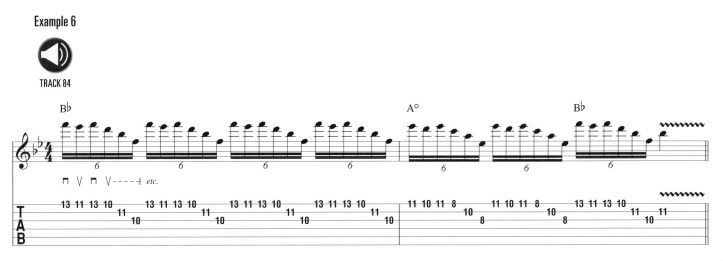

And although strings 3–1 are the most commonly used for these arpeggio shapes, the other string groups do see some action as well. In this example, we're playing on the 5–3 string group exclusively, answering an ascending root-position arpeggio sweep up to the 7th of each chord with a descending three-notes-per-string scale. Every note is picked here, and it all lays out neatly for the economy picker.

Example 7

TRACK 85

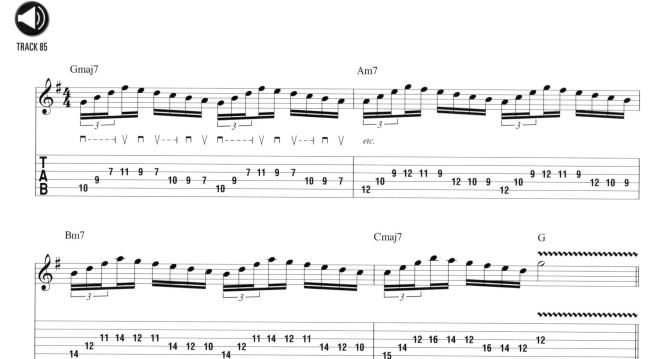

Four-String Sweeps

Four-string sweeps are an interesting thing because they trip a lot of people up when they try to use them the same way as three-note sweeps (i.e., ascending downstroke sweeps with an added note on top). The prototypical four-note version of the three-string triplet arpeggio pattern is played in 16th notes and looks something like this:

Example 8

TRACK 86

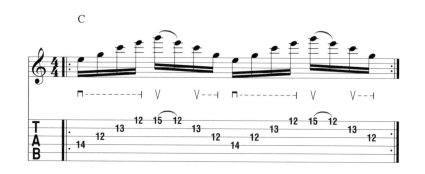

Ascending isn't much different than the three-note version; you just have to sweep through one more string, which is no biggie. But descending is usually the trouble spot for most people. Specifically, it's going from the last note of beats 2 and 4 to the first note of beats 3 and 1 (when repeating). You have to sweep upward through strings 2 and 3, then hop over string 4 in order to start sweeping down again. This seems to be significantly more difficult for most people (it certainly is for me) than the three-string version, and it's probably why you don't hear this type of thing nearly as much.

But! It is learnable with practice. It's all a matter of timing—knowing when to start lifting the pick in order to clear string 4 during the descent. Following is a little etude that works several different shapes while using this technique. Work it slowly at first, imagining yourself efficiently clearing that fourth string every time like a hurdler. Be sure to notice the picking at the very end, at which point we resolve the line with a downstroke sweep.

Example 9

TRACK 87

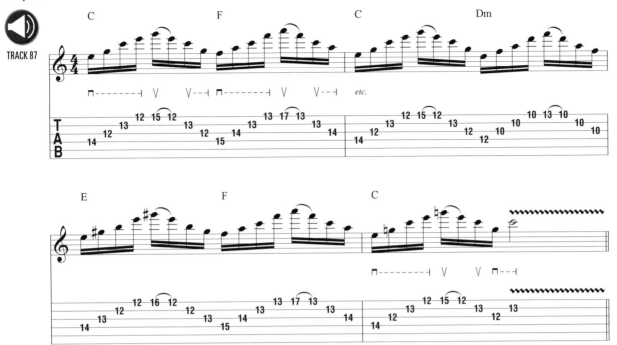

One reason that four-string sweeps aren't as common as, say, five-string sweeps, is that you can't just add a note to the bottom string to make it an even rhythmic pattern. We'll see in a bit that, with five-string arpeggios, you can create a nice triplet/sextuplet-based pattern by simply adding a note to the low string. This added note on the low string of the shape is critical because it allows you to avoid that awkward hop that you have to do in Examples 8 and 9.

For example, if we were to simply add a note (D) to string 4 in Example 8, we'd end up with groups of five:

Example 10

TRACK 88

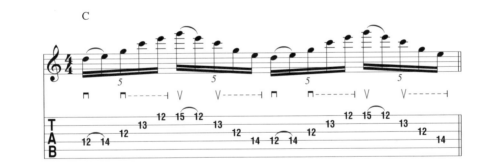

You can see how, by adding this note, we're allowed to continue our upward sweep through string 4. While this is easier to play for most people, it's not very common because, well, groups of five generally aren't very common. It's not that it doesn't sound great; it's just not what most people gravitate towards.

One way to rectify this is to add *two* notes to string 4. This will create groups of six, so it's easily applied to triplets, sextuplets, or 16th notes, creating a syncopated feel in the latter. Here, we add a low C (root) note below the D on string 4 and play the pattern in triplets:

Example 11

TRACK 89

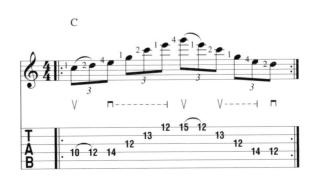

This is a viable option for getting a useful pattern out of these four-string arpeggio shapes. And, of course, you can adapt this idea to minor chords as well. Here's the same idea for a Dm chord:

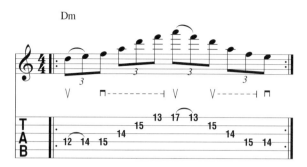

And you can turn the idea on its head, playing only two notes on string 4 but having three notes on string 1. Here's a demonstration of that idea:

Example 12

TRACK 90

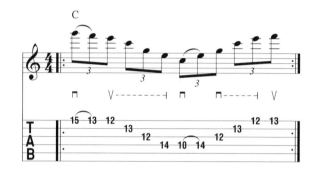

Simply put, there are plenty of ways to make four-string sweeps usable if you just put a little thought into it.

Five- and Six-String Sweeps

These are the mega-sweeps—the ones that tend to get really insane-sounding when played at dizzying speeds, as they often are in the hands of people like Frank Gambale, Michael Angelo Batio, and Marshall Harrison. The same basic logic that applied to four-string sweeps also applies here: people generally add a note (or notes) to the bottom string in order to avoid the awkward hop.

Five-string shapes lay out nicely as six-note groupings. A very common application of this is a minor-chord arpeggio that starts from the fifth-string root, such as this one in A minor:

Example 13

TRACK 91

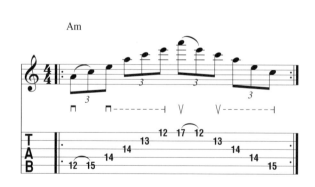

The hardest part about this shape is rolling your ring finger across strings 4 and 3. It's not too bad when you're ascending, but when you're descending, you have to be very precise with the finger placement; otherwise, you can end up sounding the C♯ note at fret 14 of string 2 while you're flattening out that ring finger. If I haven't played this shape in a while, I usually find that happening once or twice before I get a handle on it again.

A major version of this shape would look like this:

Example 14

TRACK 92

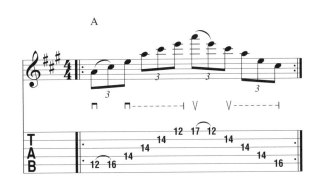

And the most difficult aspect of that shape is making all the notes on strings 4–2 distinct and separate. Rolling your finger (either your middle or ring) across three strings and keeping the notes from ringing together is no easy task.

It's also common to play these shapes in second-inversion form, which has the 5th on the bottom. Here's what that would look like for Am and A:

Example 15A

TRACK 93

Example 15B

TRACK 94

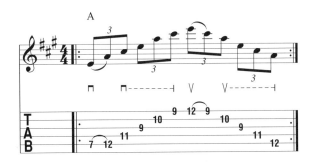

These are a little more stretchy on the low end, but you don't have to roll any fingers, so it's easier to keep all the notes clean (for me, at least!).

Let's play through a few little arpeggio exercises to get these forms under our fingers. This first one makes use of some "borrowed chords" in C major. We have a second-inversion C major arpeggio and root-position A♭ and B♭ arpeggios.

Example 16

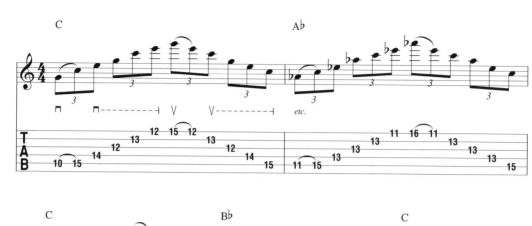

And here's another take on the five-string shape, demonstrating what a little imagination can do. Playing 16th notes here, we won't add a note to the bottom string until the very end of the measure, yet we're playing full, five-string sweeps in both directions. The same G major pattern is modified to fit the Em harmony in measure 2. The Em shape is a little stretchy, so be sure to keep the thumb behind the neck.

Example 17

Six-string shapes aren't as common as the five-string ones, simply because they suffer the same problem as the four-string shapes. It's difficult to sweep them with only one note on the bottom string, and adding a note to it doesn't produce a common grouping. If we add a note to the bottom string and add one to the top, as we did with our three- and five-string sweeps, we'll get a grouping of *seven*, which is arguably even weirder than five.

Example 18

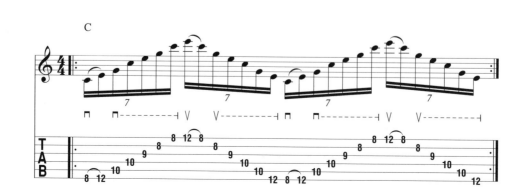

And this is not to mention the fact that you have two different spots where you have to roll a finger: strings 5–4 and strings 2–1.

Adding another note to string 6 will create an eight-note grouping, which will fit perfectly into 16th notes:

Example 19

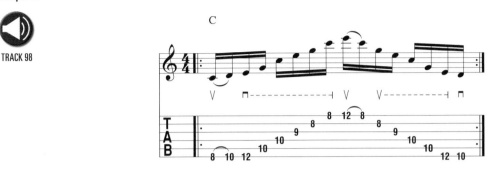

TRACK 98

Still, it's quite a handful for both hands and is not for the faint of heart. If you're intrepid in your sweeping, however, you can find many variations that will make the six-string shapes plenty useful. Here's one such idea in which we omit a note from each direction in order to create a six-note grouping. It's a bit unclear in the music, but when repeating this phrase, you would simply continue the upward sweep all the way through string 6.

Example 20

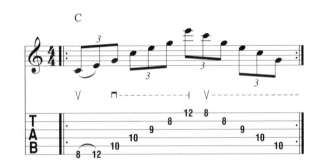

TRACK 99

When you combine three-, four-, five-, and six-string shapes, the world is your sweeping oyster!

Licks

Let's check out some of these extended sweeps in action. This first one is an alternate take on the three-string sweep. We're adding a note to the bottom string to create an eight-note group that's played in 16th notes. Although, technically, we're never sweeping through three strings at once, it sounds as though we are.

Lick 1

TRACK 100

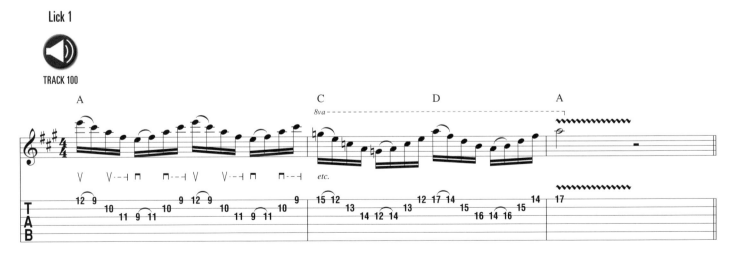

And here's yet another take on the three-string sweep, this time on strings 4–2. We're sweeping three downstrokes in a row and then picking up on string 2 to play seventh-chord arpeggios for Fmaj7 and Dm7. For the C chord, we maintain the same technique but replace the 7th on string 2 with a 6th for a C6 sound. It will help to use a forward pick slant in measures 1–3, as that will make the jump from string 2 back to string 4 easier. In measure 4, we make use of a four-string sweep over a G chord to bring the lick to a close.

Lick 2

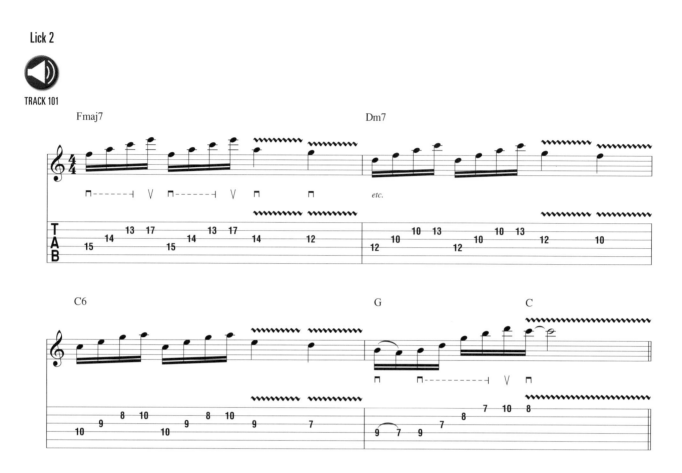

TRACK 101

This lick is based on the five-string shapes, but I've added a bit of scalar interplay to mix it up as well. After sweeping through one octave of an Am shape with downstrokes, we play some angular-sounding melodies on strings 2 and 1 before descending back through Am with upstroke sweeps. For the F chord in measure 2, I start by transposing the line from measure 1. To save it from sounding too predictable though, I break off at the end of measure 2 and descend the A minor scale using the "forward pick-slanting cheat" method that we covered in Chapter 6.

Lick 3

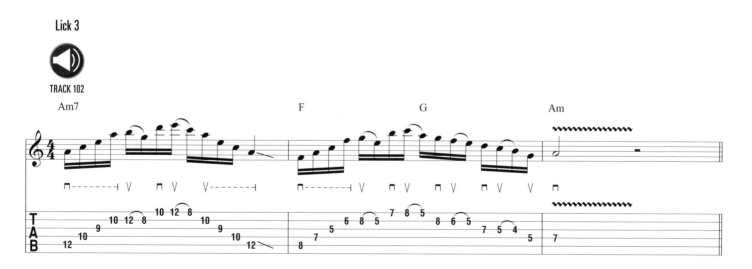

TRACK 102

We'll finish off with a barn-burner from G Dorian. We're playing through all six strings here, but we're adding several notes along the way to mix it up. The tonality is interesting because we're mixing two different arpeggio sounds: Gm7 on the bottom and C7 on the top. Taken altogether, it creates kind of a Gm13 sound against the harmony. In measure 2, after ascending in similar fashion, we bring the phrase to a close with some scalar economy picking. There's nothing terribly hard here, but at this tempo, your pinky will get quite a workout during those arpeggios.

Lick 4

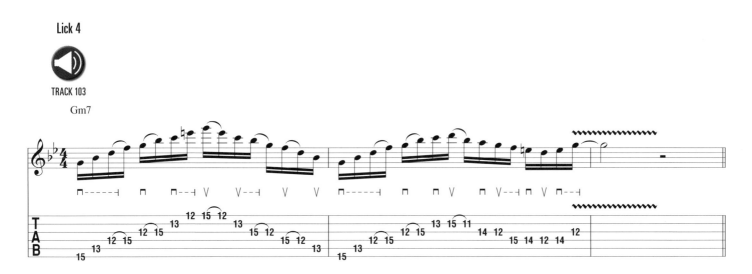

TRACK 103

Gm7

WHAT YOU LEARNED

- Sweep picking is the fastest way to play arpeggios with a pick. (You could argue that tapping is probably just as fast, but that's another topic.)

- Three-string triadic sweeps are most commonly applied to strings 3–1, in ascending fashion.

- A note on the top string, usually an octave above the lowest note, is often added to a three-string sweep to create a group of six when running straight up and down the shape.

- Four-string shapes are not as common as three-string shapes because of an awkward string hop that needs to be executed over the bottom string when descending. You can get around this by adding a note or two to the bottom string.

- Notes can be added to the top or bottom strings of three-, four-, five-, or six-string shapes to create variation in rhythm and/or melody.

- Legato moves are often employed when extra notes are added on top or bottom of an arpeggio shape to "right the ship" in the picking hand for repeating phrases.

SECTION 3: THE BIG PICTURE
CHAPTER 8 – LICKS AND TRICKS OF THE MASTERS

Now that you've learned the ins and outs of the technique, let's take a look at some specific ways that the masters use it in their lead playing. It's very interesting how everyone can take what they want from the concept and exploit it in their own unique way.

Eric Johnson

As mentioned previously, Eric is a forward pick-slanter and only uses economy picking on downstrokes during his fast playing. The only real exception to this is that sometimes he will quickly rake, or "smear," through a chord shape with an upstroke, but it's not something he does in time or in a repeated fashion.

Here's a classic Eric move using an Fm7 arpeggio shape, which he makes sound completely effortless. One of the things that Eric has absolutely mastered (and there are many) is the ability to seamlessly transition between sweeping and alternate picking. Beat 3 of this phrase is a perfect example. After sweeping from string 3 to string 2 with a downstroke, you need to resume alternate picking for the final four notes of the ascent without missing a beat. An exercise that I found particularly helpful in this regard is to start from that E♭ note on beat 3 (fret 16, string 2) *with your pick already touching the string*, ready to pick down. Play those four notes—E♭, F, A♭, C—over and over, beginning with your pick pre-planted that way each time. This really helped me make that transition smoother.

Lick 1

TRACK 104

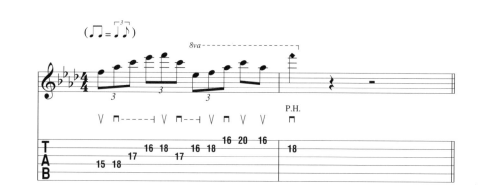

This is another Eric classic: descending groups of five through a minor pentatonic scale. In this case, we're in C minor. The picking pattern is down-up-down-up-down for each beat, and you'll sweep into the first note of each subsequent beat. It will take a bit of time to get the feel for quintuplets if you're not used to them!

Lick 2

TRACK 105

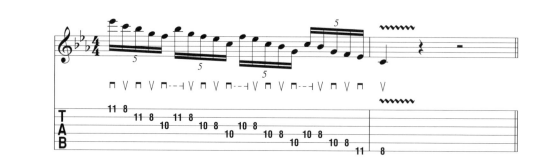

Zakk Wylde

Zakk originally made a name for himself when he joined Ozzy's band at the tender age of 20, and he's been kicking ass and taking names ever since. Like Eric, Zakk can flat out shred the living daylight out of the pentatonic scale. Coincidentally, he's also a forward pick-slanter and uses economy picking primarily on downstrokes. First up is an example of how Zakk will use the repetitive three-note-pattern concept that we talked about in Chapter 4. Use a forward pick slant, and your pick can remain that way throughout the lick. Notice how he mixes F♯ minor pentatonic ideas (measure 1) with arpeggios (C♯m and D, measures 2 and 3, respectively). We have to alternate pick the first three notes of measures 2 and 3 to right the ship, but other than that, we're picking down-down-up throughout. If you wanted to, you could just employ an upward sweep for the last two notes in measures 1 and 2 instead, which would eliminate alternate picking altogether.

Lick 3

TRACK 106

Zakk's also a master of the speedy repetitive lick—usually a pentatonic one—thrown into a solo to quickly melt a face or two. Here's an example of that idea in D minor. We're playing the same exact thing in two different positions, yet all the notes stem from D minor pentatonic.

Lick 4

TRACK 107

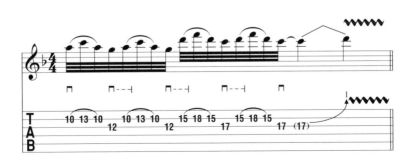

Frank Gambale

One of the undisputed masters and greatest proponents of the economy technique, it's safe to say that Frank Gambale may be the most well-known economy picker out there. What's even more impressive is that he's not just playing rock licks (although he certainly can!), but sophisticated jazz fusion lines that can span the neck as if it's child's play. Equally skilled at arpeggios and scalar playing, his technique seems to be limited only by his imagination.

Here's a very Frank-sounding approach to a six-string dominant seventh arpeggio (in this case, F7) in which every note is picked and sweeps are used throughout. He accomplishes this by skipping the 7th tone in the second octave during both the ascent and the descent. There's a bit of a fret-hand stretch, but at this spot on the neck, it's certainly manageable.

Lick 5

TRACK 108

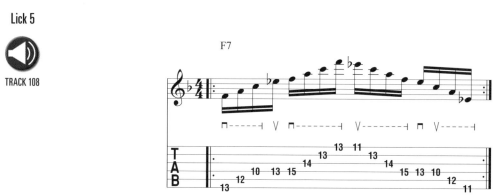

Frank also has a very clever way of sweeping through pentatonic scales: alternating three notes and one note. Here's how that might look in a D minor pentatonic scale. Again, the fret hand is a bit stretchy, but the picking mechanics are 100% efficient. Although Frank doesn't have terribly long fingers (such as Eric Johnson or Steve Vai), he still manages these types of stretches and more without any trouble at all.

Lick 6

TRACK 109

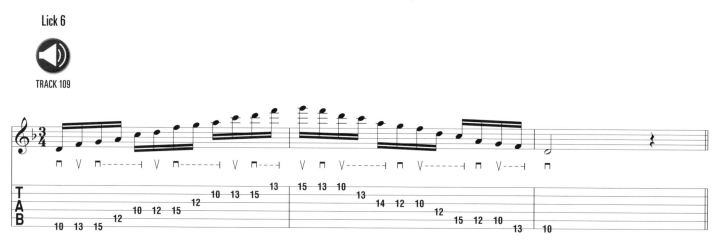

Marshall Harrison

If there's anyone to possibly challenge Frank for supreme economy picker of our time, it's probably Marshall. Watching him play makes you think anyone could do it. His pick hand simply glides in and out of the strings like butter, and there's no sense of difficulty or effort present at all. As with Frank, Marshall employs sweeping in both directions with equal finesse to scales, arpeggios, and anything in between. He's also a big proponent of what's becoming known as "swybrid picking," which is a combination of sweep picking and hybrid picking (i.e., using the pick and a pick-hand finger).

Here's an example of Marshall's creative problem-solving with economy picking. We're playing a descending four-note sequence in C major here, but Marshall shifts up in position every two beats. This creates a repeatable picking pattern that maximizes sweeping potential.

Lick 7

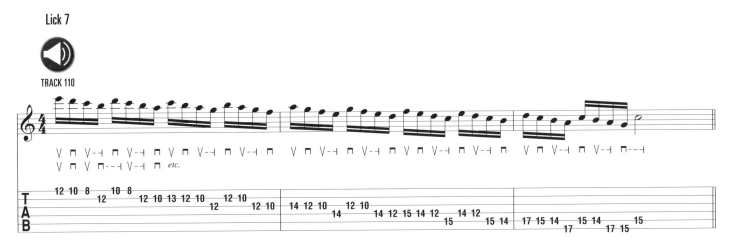

As a somewhat different take on Frank's seventh-chord arpeggio sweeps, here's how Marshall will sometimes approach a dominant seventh arpeggio. It still alternates three notes and one note per string, but it's doing so on different degrees of the arpeggio. Here, Marshall will play the ♭7th, root, and 3rd on one string and then place the 5th on its own. This process then repeats an octave higher and resolves to the 3rd (C♯) of an A chord. At higher positions on the neck such as these, you can get away with simply stretching for the ♭7th–root–3rd run. On lower positions, however, you may have to shift up a bit to grab the 3rd, which makes it much more difficult to play quickly.

Lick 8

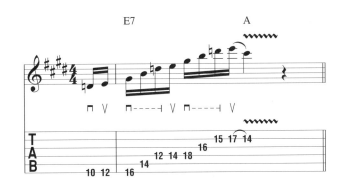

Jason Becker

When it came to sweep picking arpeggios in the neo-classical style, few did it better than Jason. He scaled up and down mountainous multiple-octave shapes as if he were born to do it. One of the interesting facets of his style was the way he would connect the octaves within an arpeggio lick. He may use one fingering for the first time through an octave but a different one the second time through in order to gain access to a higher range. The following D major arpeggio phrase demonstrates that. First, we climb up to a D note on string 2, fret 15 before coming back down. The second time through, however, we start at the A note (instead of the low D) in preparation for a higher climb. Therefore, we continue up through the D at fret 10, string 1 so that we can climb up to F♯ on the way to a shift up to a high A at fret 17 with the pinky, which puts us in the final destination for the lick. In retrospect, we can see that by playing the D at fret 15, string 2 the first time, we're able to employ a pull-off, which makes it easier on the picking hand.

Lick 9

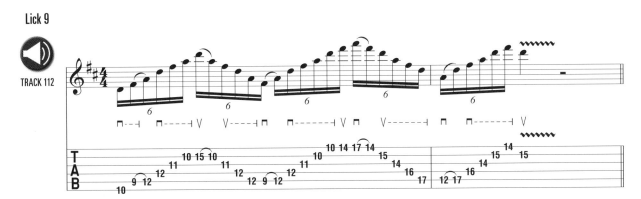

Yngwie Malmsteen

As mentioned previously, Yngwie only employs economy picking with downstrokes, most likely due to his pick angle, which remains fairly constant. This means that the mechanics of his technique are similar to Zakk and Eric, but he achieves very different results because of what he chooses to play and his penchant for classical-sounding licks.

Here's an example of how he uses economy picking for ascending scalar passages. Note that he purposefully does not sweep upward from string 5 to string 6 after the fifth note (E at fret 7 of string 5) even though he could, because the pick is moving toward string 6. This is completely purposeful, however, because by using a downstroke on the second note of beat 2 (on string 6), he's able to sweep down to string 5, which aligns with his forward pick slant. Once he reaches the second D note on string 5 (beat 2.5), the rest of the lick follows the economy picking rule of odd numbers of notes to keep going in the same direction. He has three notes on string 5, seven notes on string 4, and three notes each on strings 3–1.

Lick 10

TRACK 113

And here's Yngwie's classic take on the diminished seventh arpeggio, which uses a three-string downward sweep. And just like the half-whole diminished scale, which we looked at in Lick 3 of Chapter 5, the diminished seventh arpeggio is symmetrical, too. You can move the shape in minor 3rd intervals, and you'll be playing all four of the same notes, just in a different inversion. And that's exactly the way Yngwie uses it. The picking pattern for each six-note grouping is up-pull-up-down-down-down.

Lick 11

TRACK 114

Jeff Loomis

Although Jeff spends a good deal of time alternate picking his aggressive scalar runs, when he throws in an economy picking run, it seems just as natural to him. One of his favorite economy picking licks makes use of the diminished scale. Whereas the half-whole diminished scale starts with a half step, the *diminished scale* alternates whole steps and half steps, but it starts with a *whole* step. (Sometimes to avoid confusion, the diminished scale is referred to as the "whole-half diminished scale.") Here's an example demonstrating that, from the G diminished scale. Every note is picked here, which means that you'll have to use alternate picking a few times during the string crosses, but most of them use economy picking.

Lick 12

TRACK 115

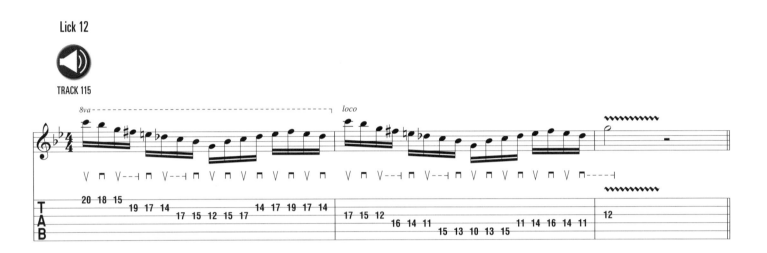

And here's an example of Jeff's shredtastic arpeggio sweeping. He uses a seven-string guitar, but this is arranged for six-string. It's very similar to what he would do, but it doesn't dip down quite as far before coming back up. To say that Jeff blazes through this is a gross understatement, but the scariest part of all is the stuff at the bottom. Whereas most people would employ some legato moves at some point, he *alternate picks* through all of those awkward string crosses before beginning to sweep downward for the ascent. I'll be straight up with you: I can't come close to Jeff's speed on this lick, so my audio demo is hardly representative of what the real thing sounds like!

Lick 13

TRACK 116

CHAPTER 9 – FULL SOLO EXAMPLES

Congratulations on making it this far! By now, your economy picking chops should be in pretty darn good shape and you're ready to tackle the extended licks in these four solos. I've made sure to incorporate just about everything we've covered at one point or another, so if you skipped over anything, now's your last chance to go back and learn it!

SOLO 1

TRACK 117

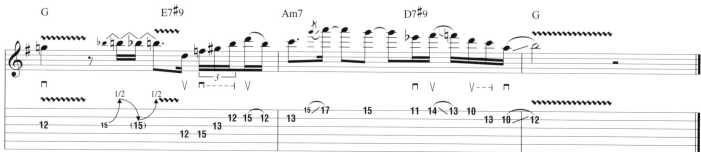

SOLO 2

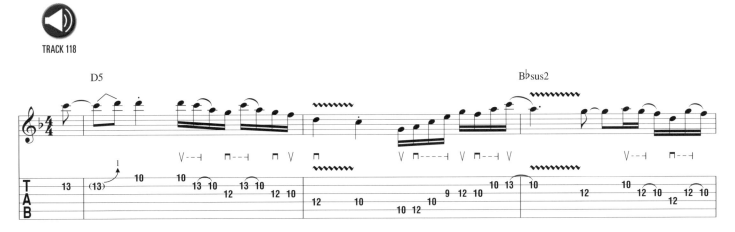

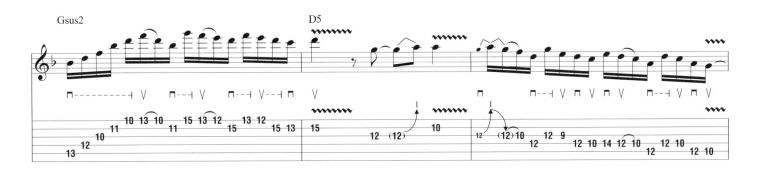

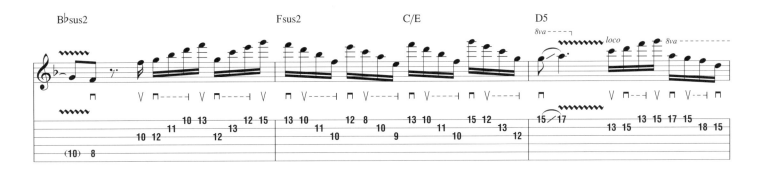

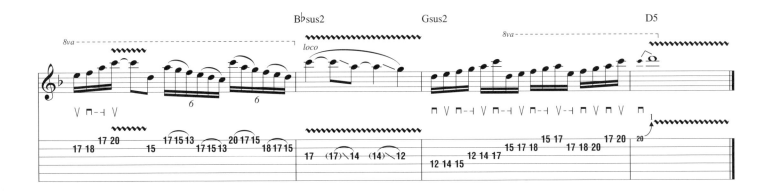

SOLO 3

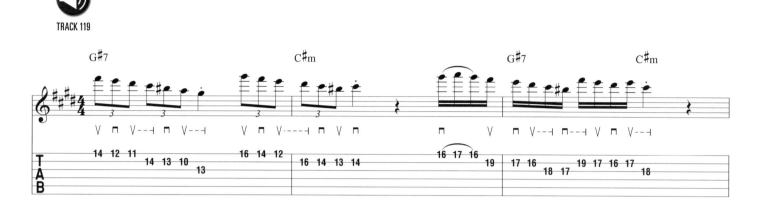

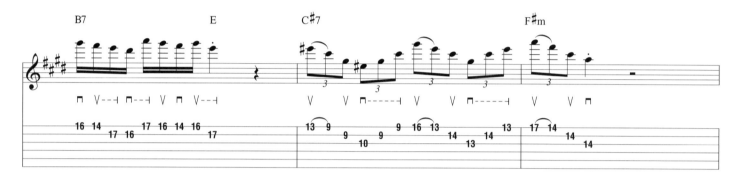

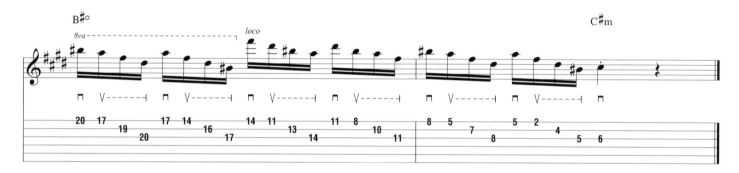

SOLO 4

TRACK 120

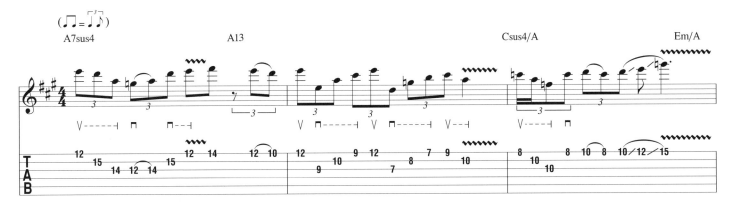

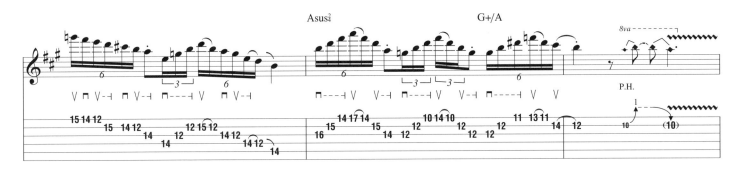

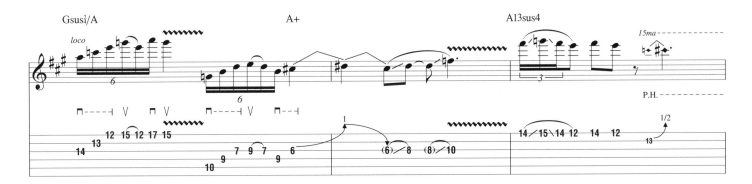

AFTERWORD

And now it's time to say goodbye. We've covered a lot of ground, and I hope you've enjoyed the journey. Remember that, while you certainly now have a strong foundation, this is hardly the extent of the possibilities for economy picking. Players are always finding new ways to implement the technique by moving a note to a different string, adding a note here, subtracting one there, etc. So keep on the lookout for opportunities; often new technical breakthroughs can spur an entire new breed of musical ideas.

I'll offer these final bits of advice:

- **Try to come up with your own variations of the examples in this book:** change a note, change the scale, try it backwards, etc. The possibilities are almost infinite. While some ideas won't lead anywhere, it's a good bet that many will.

- **Use… a… metronome:** Seriously.

- **Transcribe other instruments:** Learn a piano, trumpet, or sax solo from a jazz record and arrange it for guitar, using economy picking when possible. Learn a fiddle solo from a country tune. How about a synth solo from a '70s fusion album? All of these things can be incredible eye-opening experiences, as you're most likely going to be playing things you've never played before.

- **Set short-term goals:** This can help you stay focused on improving and expanding your repertoire instead of falling into the same old patterns.

- **Play with other musicians:** There's no substitute for getting together with real people and jamming. You're most likely going to learn something from almost every person you play with. Granted, sometimes it may be what you *don't want to do*, but those lessons are valuable, too! But plenty of times, you'll just find that other people have a different way of looking at things, and it expands your own horizons.

Be sure to check out the Appendixes that follow. You'll find scale diagrams, arpeggio diagrams, and lots of backing tracks for you to jam along with while trying out your new skills. Good luck!

APPENDIX

Welcome to the Appendix. Won't you stay awhile?

Scale Diagrams

Here are the most common scales, presented here with a C tonic note. Since all of the scale forms are moveable (i.e., they don't contain any open strings), you can transpose them to any key. The seven-note diatonic scales and modes are presented in three-notes-per-string fashion to facilitate the economy technique.

C Major (Ionian)
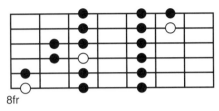
8fr

C Dorian
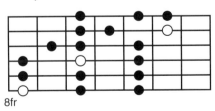
8fr

C Phrygian
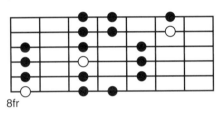
8fr

C Lydian
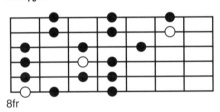
8fr

C Mixolydian
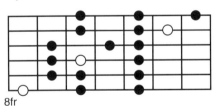
8fr

C Minor (Aeolian)
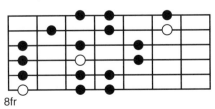
8fr

C Locrian
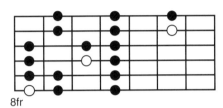
8fr

C Harmonic Minor
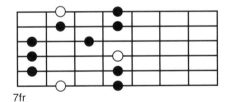
8fr

C Melodic Minor
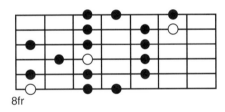
8fr

C Major Pentatonic
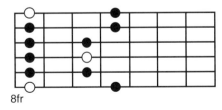
7fr

C Minor Pentatonic
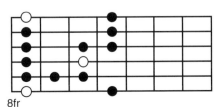
8fr

C Blues

8fr

C Diminished (Whole-Half)

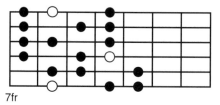

7fr

C Half-Whole Diminished

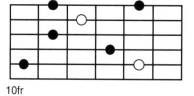

7fr

Arpeggio Diagrams

Here you'll find several options for triad and seventh-chord arpeggios, presented with a C root. Note that you can find the three- or four-string forms embedded within these extended forms.

C Major Triad

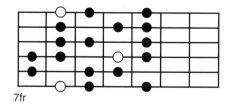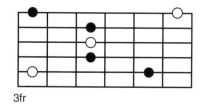

8fr   10fr   3fr

C Minor Triad

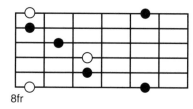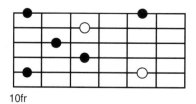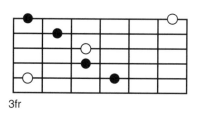

8fr   10fr   3fr

C Augmented Triad

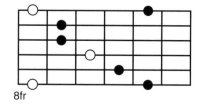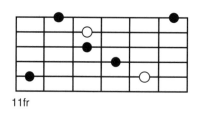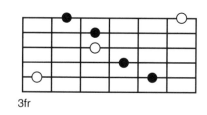

8fr   11fr   3fr

C Diminished Triad

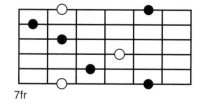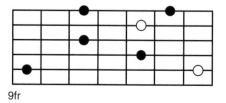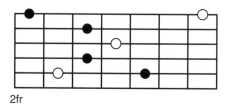

7fr   9fr   2fr

Cmaj7

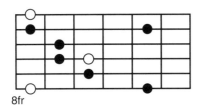

8fr

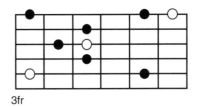

3fr

Cm7

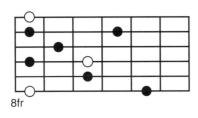

8fr

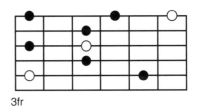

3fr

C7

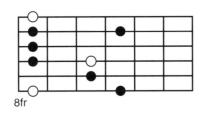

8fr

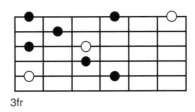

3fr

Cm7♭5

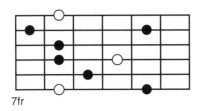

7fr

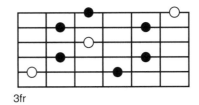

3fr

C°7

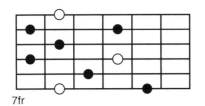

7fr

3fr

Jam Tracks

Here are several backing tracks in different styles. You can use them to practice your new economy picking licks. I've included scale suggestions for each one.

Major and Minor Diatonic Progressions

Progression #1: I–IV in C major (C major scale)

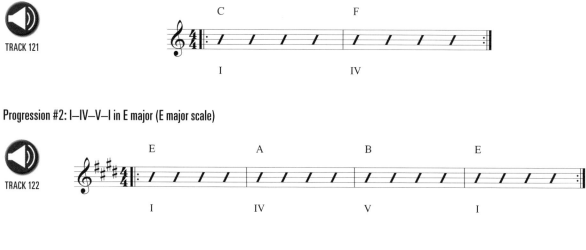

Progression #2: I–IV–V–I in E major (E major scale)

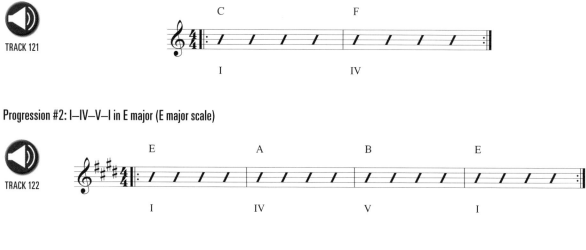

Progression #3: I–V–vi–IV in D major (D major scale)

Progression #4: i–♭VI–♭VII–i in C minor (C minor scale)

Major and Minor Progressions with Non-Diatonic Chords

Progression #5: I–I7–IV–iv in G major (I, IV: G major scale; I7: G Mixolydian; iv: G minor scale)

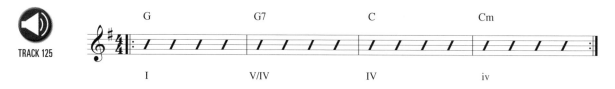

Progression #6: I–♭VI–♭VII–IV in B major (I, IV: B major scale; ♭VI, ♭VII: B minor scale)

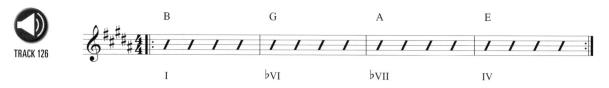

Progression #7: i–♭VII–IV–V in A minor (i, ♭VII: A minor scale; IV: A Dorian; V: A harmonic minor)

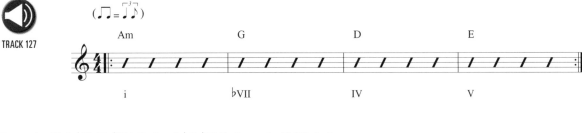

Progression #8: i–♭III–IV–♭VI in E minor (i, ♭III, ♭VI: E minor scale; IV: E Dorian)

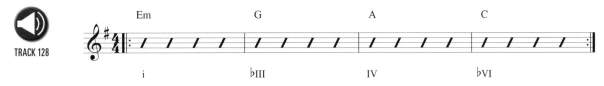

Modal Progressions

Progression #9: I–♭VII–IV in E major (E Mixolydian)

Progression #10: i–♭VII–IV–i in B minor (B Dorian)

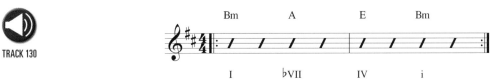

Progression #11: i–IV in D minor (D Dorian)

Blues Progressions

Progression #12: 12-bar blues shuffle in A major

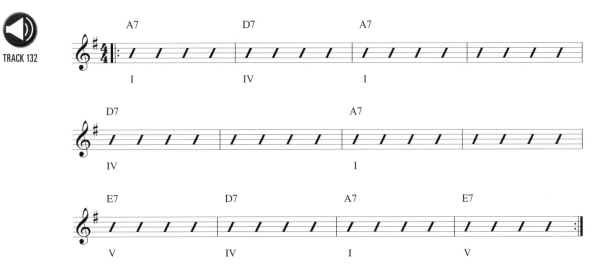

Progression #13: funky 12-bar blues in C major

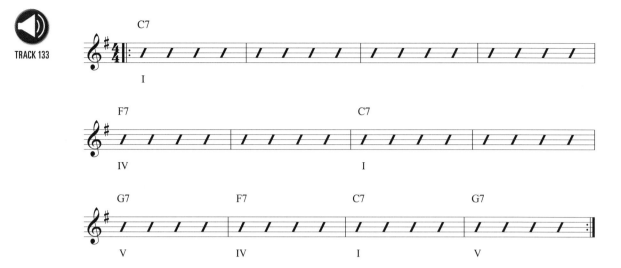

Progression #14: rock-style 12-bar blues in B minor

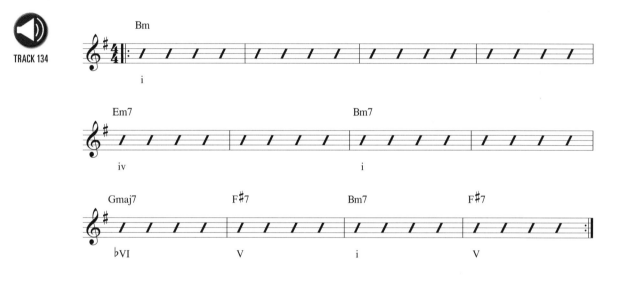

Progression #15: slow 12-bar blues shuffle in E minor

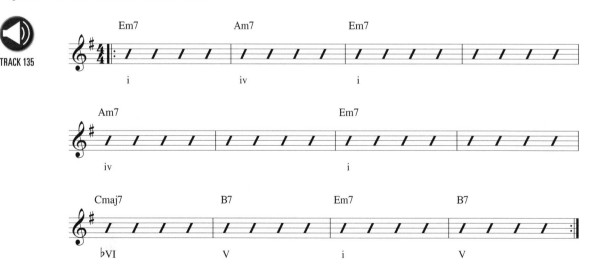